CHANGING THE GAME

THE NEW WAY TO SELL

LARRY WILSON
WITH HERSCH WILSON

SIMON AND SCHUSTER
NEW YORK · LONDON · TORONTO · SYDNEY · TOKYO

Copyright © 1987 by Larry Wilson
All rights reserved
including the right of reproduction
in whole or in part in any form.
Published by Simon and Schuster
A Division of Simon & Schuster, Inc.
Simon & Schuster Building
Rockefeller Center
1230 Avenue of the Americas
New York, NY 10020
SIMON AND SCHUSTER and colophon are registered trademarks
of Simon & Schuster, Inc.

Designed by Irving Perkins Associates
Manufactured in the United States of America

2   3   4   5   6   7   8   9   10

Library of Congress Cataloging in Publication Data

Wilson, Larry.
Changing the game.

Includes index.
1. Selling.   I. Wilson, Hersch.   II. Title.
HF5438.25.W299   1987   658.8′5   87-12900
ISBN 0-671-61313-8

The purpose of this book is to help salespeople everywhere discover the power, courage and creativity they have been given, and to use them in the service of making a difference and creating a better world.

ACKNOWLEDGMENTS

Like most endeavors I've been involved with in my life, this book was a result of powerful teamwork. Over fifty people gave of their time, energy and, most important, their honesty and creativity in order to bring this book to you.

First off, two people who lived with this book for one year, all over the world, through countless interviews and countless drafts, were my co-author and son, Hersch Wilson, and our irrepressible interviewer, friend and writer Ronn Lehmann.

For shaping the book, guiding us, and never being satisfied with anything less than the best we could do, I'd like to thank Bob Bender, our editor at Simon and Schuster, and Jonathan Lazear, my agent in Minneapolis.

For their expertise in sales and sales training, their ideas, patience and willingness to share, I'd like to thank George Ainsworth-Land, Akiko Shiotsu, Elizabeth Adams and Tom Haller; and in our Japan office Shozo Mori, Hirkoi Iizuka and Yoshimichi Ueno.

Other people who gave their ideas and time were Bill Payne, Joan Ward, Willis Harman, Hank Marban of IBM and Roy Yamahiro of Federal Express.

Next I'd like to thank the salespeople we interviewed whose voices you'll hear in this book: Larry Mann of Aetna, Charles Breckenridge of Cray Research, Eric Carlson of Du Pont, Kathy Monthei of Delta Dental Plan of California, Alan Braslow of Five Technologies, Don Walker of Wilson Learning Corporation, Ann Ramsay Spinazzola of NorthWestern

Mutual, Diane Flis of Buick, Eileen Tertocha of Skipper Morrison Realtors in Atlanta and Jay Mesinger of Mesinger and Associates in Houston.

Then there is the team who worked on the book. I'd especially like to thank Jill Wenburg for her endless patience and enthusiasm while transcribing hours of taped interviews. I'd also like to thank Jody Kirk, Laurie Edwards-Wilson and, in Tokyo, Tomoko Inamoto, for their help.

There is one company that needs to be acknowledged, for without it this book would not have been written. That company is Federal Express. "Fed Ex" gave us the gift of being able to write this book in God's country, rural northern New Mexico, yet being always only an overnight delivery away from Simon and Schuster in New York.

Finally, I must acknowledge that hundreds of pages, from the first to the final draft, were written on what I think is one of the most important inventions of this half century—the personal computer. Ronn Lehmann, our research writer, worked on an IBM PC and Hersch Wilson and I worked on Apple Computer MacIntoshes without any glitches, problems or even the loss of one page of information. Concerning "PCs," we went from being dubious in the beginning to becoming fanatic supporters by the final draft.

To all, thank you for help and contributions.

CONTENTS

Acknowledgments   7
Author's Note   13

PART I The Changing Game of Selling

CHAPTER 1 *What This Book Is All About*   18
CHAPTER 2 *Understanding the New Game*   29
CHAPTER 3 *The Rules of the New Game*   52
CHAPTER 4 *The Game Changers*   77

PART II Winning the New Game of Selling

CHAPTER 5 STP NO. 1: *You Cannot Fail*   102
CHAPTER 6 STP NO. 2: *Selling on Purpose: Helping Others Get What They Want*   124
CHAPTER 7 STP NO. 3: *Creating with Vision*   141
CHAPTER 8 STP NO. 4: *Leading the Team*   160
CHAPTER 9 STP NO. 5: *Partnering*   180
CHAPTER 10 STP NO. 6: *Value Added*   198
CHAPTER 11 STP NO. 7: *Applying the Principle of Leverage*   223

PART III Women, Managers, and the New Game

CHAPTER 12 *The Natural Superiority of Women*   249
CHAPTER 13 *Managing the High Performance Sales Team*   261
Afterword *Journey's End*   277
Index   281

AUTHOR'S NOTE

A few words about how I came to write this book. For me, it's the capstone of thirty years of selling, speaking about selling, and training hundreds of thousands of salespeople at Wilson Learning Corporation, the company I founded in 1964.

In that thirty years, we've seen dramatic changes in selling. The profession has left behind it the image of Willy Loman in *Death of a Salesman* and Harold Hill in *The Music Man* and is emerging as one of the most sophisticated, vital, challenging and important roles in business today. Unquestionably, today selling is one of the key activities that moves the economy forward, that keeps the pie growing.

As a profession, it's clear to me, selling is one of the few livelihoods in our economy where the entrepreneurial spirit is alive and well. Salespeople, the best and the brightest, *think* differently from others. They think like entrepreneurs, because that's what they are, and that is what is so exciting about selling.

In large part, then, this book is about that excitement—the excitement of the possibilities and the promises that selling has to offer. For me personally, as I look ahead at the next thirty years, whether I'm wearing the hat of CEO, speaker or writer, selling is what I will always be doing because of the promise and the possibilities.

LARRY WILSON
The Pecos River Learning Center
Santa Fe, New Mexico
Christmas 1986

PART I

THE CHANGING GAME
OF SELLING

A GAME

A set of rules completely specifying the goal of the game and the roles of the participants, including the permissible actions of and information available to each participant, the criteria for establishing progress, the probabilities with which random events may occur, the criteria for termination of the game, and the distribution of payoffs. Finally, the rules specify why the game is being played.

CHAPTER 1

WHAT THIS BOOK
IS ALL ABOUT

Business today is terrific. Couldn't be better. Most exciting, exhilarating, demanding, rewarding time of my life. First of all, there are so so many people who need our services. It's just incredible to me. I could literally work eight days a week, thirty-six hours a day. There's that much to do, that many prospects to see, that many people who need our services.

LARRY MANN, Aetna Life and Casualty,
Los Angeles, California

According to a lot of people, we've gone through some rough times. We've gone through a recession. And I didn't recognize that when it was going on. I guess I was just so hungry that I just broke through that and went out and looked for business.

I never dreamed that I would be this successful in selling. I never dreamed that when I was twenty-four I'd own a $125,000 house on a lake. I never dreamed that I would be one of the top car salespeople in the nation. What's happened is way beyond anything that I

18

ever thought of. I'm thirty now, and by the time I'm thirty-five I hope to have my own dealership.
DIANE FLIS, Tamaroff Buick,
Detroit, Michigan

I think that the marketplace for our business is a gold mine. All the caring and effort is paying off. Referrals alone are taking up 80 percent of my time. Business is better than ever!
ALAN BRASLOW, Five Technologies,
Woodcliff, New Jersey

It's almost frightening to me to see myself now. I feel like I've just let go of the reins, I've let loose of trying to control my clients, and business is just pouring in the door. It's ridiculous, it's nuts.
KATHY MONTHEI, Delta Dental Plan of California,
Oakland, California

I know that I'll never retire. I know I won't. There are people in my insurance study group that are in their eighties. You just don't have to retire when you're doing something meaningful. I'm just too gung-ho. And the market's never gone flat for me. It's the most steady industry that I can think of.
ANN SPINAZZOLA, NorthWestern Mutual Life,
Dallas, Texas

This is going to be the perfect substitute for my music —that's what I thought when I started my real-estate career thirteen years ago. Today, after ten consecutive years in the million-dollar club and as one of Atlanta's top twenty residential realtors (in a city of over seven thousand real-estate agents), I know I was right! As an entertainer, I was in business to please people, and essentially that's the prime element in selling real estate.

> EILEEN TERTOCHA, Skipper Morrison Realtors,
> Atlanta, Georgia

How would you like to own some of that excitement about selling? And not only have the success that these people are talking about, but also the sense of fulfillment that is so apparent? Further, how would you like to feel like that in the midst of one of the most turbulent, unpredictable phases in business and selling history?

Helping you discover the possibilities, those kinds of feelings, helping you see selling through the eyes of these salespeople, is the goal of this book.

Now, that's a lot to ask of a book. So I need to request something of you first. The favor is this: Suspend—for the duration—all the notions, ideas and beliefs that you have about selling. For the time it takes you to read this book, put aside all the definitions of selling, of customers, of products and services that you grew up with, that your sales manager gave you, or that you've inherited from your organization.

I'm asking you for this favor because we're going to start with a clean sheet of paper and reinvent our profession.

NEW GAME, NEW RULES

First off, it's important to understand that in selling, we don't just change what we've been doing—especially if we've been successful at it—on a whim or because it's what the "experts" recommend. In selling we change how we think, how we work and how we sell in order to stay abreast—or better yet—a little ahead of our customers. *Staying close to customers* as they change is the best reason for salespeople to change how they operate and think.

And the world of our customers, from the individual consumer to the large corporations, is experiencing radical change. The research we do at Wilson Learning Corporation, which for twenty-five years has been interviewing salespeople and their customers, together with my own personal experiences talking to salespeople from all over the world have convinced me that business, our economy and therefore our customers are going through change like we've never seen before.

In turn, these changes, the transformations occurring in our customers' worlds, are transforming selling. Everything from the personal relationship we have with customers to what we sell is changing. In the sessions we do with salespeople at the Pecos River Learning Center in Santa Fe, New Mexico, we've identified six major shifts in how selling is changing:

1. In every sale, even at the individual consumer level, there are more decision-makers involved.
2. The length of time it takes to close a sale has increased dramatically.
3. Because of the uncertainty of the times and the turbulence that we are experiencing today in business, there has been an exponential increase in random events: companies bought and sold, reorganizations, new industries and bankruptcies. All of these seemingly random events are out of the control of salespeople, yet they have a major effect on the business of selling and the mental health of salespeople.
4. Where before customers used to accept "generic" solutions and products, now they are demanding specific, "custom made" solutions. Mass market solutions are fading from the landscape because they're increasingly unacceptable to customers.
5. Customers are looking for a different, higher level,

longer term relationship with the salespeople and the companies they deal with.

6. Finally, the product solution, the features and benefits, the competitive advantage of my product over your product are no longer what customers are primarily interested in; it's no longer primarily what they are buying. We call this the death of the product solution.

Add to these the "3 Cs." Selling has become more Complicated, Competitive and Complex, and you can understand that we are talking about dramatic change.

And that is why this book is called "Changing the Game." The point is that the changes we're experiencing are so fundamental and so deep that we will not survive by just tinkering with the rules of the old game. Instead, we need to change the entire game.

THE CHANGE OPTIONS

Since this book is about changing the entire game, let's try to understand what change is, why we should change and what our change options are. There are basically three ways that individuals or organizations change.

Shock

The first type of change is through shock. Being shocked into change occurs when you are forced to change with seemingly no forewarning, or, as is more frequently the case, when we have ignored all kinds of good clues. Shock is receiving a divorce summons from your spouse's attorney and discovering that you were the last to find out. It is walking into your best client's office and finding out that you've lost the account to a competitor you've never heard of before. Being shocked into change is what happened to the American automobile industry in the midseventies when it was hit with the double blow of oil embargoes and foreign competition.

Our general response to shock is coping—trying to minimize the damage and manage the crisis. But sometimes shock kills the patient.

Evolution

The second kind of change is evolutionary. A company or an individual slowly adapts to change by following the pack. A salesperson discovers a successful approach, and pretty soon everybody else is doing it. For example, one insurance company trains its people to be full-service financial specialists, and soon everyone on the block is calling himself a financial adviser.

In the computer arena, the march from huge mainframe computers to the mini-computers and finally to the personal computer was an example of evolutionary change. Except for Apple Computer, the inventor and innovator of the PC game, most of the industry moved in lock step with one another. They adapted in incremental steps, following the crowd. Seemingly painless, seemingly prudent.

But both changing by shock and changing by evolution carry a high price. The cost of shock is easy to see. It reverberates across jobs, careers and companies. "Shocked out of existence" has been a frightening drumbeat of the last decade. All sorts of companies and industries have gone and will continue to go that route.

The cost of the evolutionary change is more subtle but just as expensive over the long term. *It's the cost of lost opportunity.* It's the price of not being on the leading edge where the new game is being played—you never catch up. Imagine if the American automobile industry had strategically thought out, predicted and prepared for the dramatic change in their industry in the early 1970s (incidentally, a perfectly reasonable possibility). The difference between what could have been and what was is the cost of lost opportunity, the cost of evolutionary change.

In business, evolutionary change can virtually mean adapting yourself right out of business. When you make evolutionary changes, you are slowly adapting to conditions. For example, if you put a frog into hot water, it will jump out before it gets scalded. But put that same frog into cold water, and slowly turn up the temperature, and the frog will simply keep adapting to the increasing heat—until it dies. It "adapts" itself to death. That can sometimes be the price of changing too slowly. You move in small increments, with no strategic vision, no strategic plan, then seemingly—all of a sudden—the water boils. The market and your customers have left you and your product behind.

Of course there are times when it's prudent to move slowly and cautiously. But today, and in the foreseeable future, where rapid, structural change is occurring and will occur all around us, it can be dangerous to move too slowly. Will Rogers said, "Even if you're on the right track, if you just sit there you're going to get run over."

But there is another change option.

The Game Change Option: Anticipation, Innovation and Strategic Change

The third option is what we call game changing. Anticipating the future, developing innovative responses and then strategically changing—changing the game. Creating the future instead of waiting for it to arrive. Peter Drucker, the "guru" of American management, was talking about this option—anticipation, innovation and strategic change—when he said, "The best way to predict the future is to create it."

It's easy to see that the number-one priority of most corporations today is this kind of strategic anticipatory change. All over the corporate landscape organizations are shedding their old skins and creating new companies, new responses to traditional markets, and even entering or creating brand-new markets. Here are some examples:

General Motors creates the Saturn project with a high reliance on automation and radically innovative labor and management contracts in order to invent a new way to manufacture cars. Then they purchase EDS, the information-processing giant, in order to plant their stake in the information management field. And they purchase Hughes Aircraft, to plant a stake in aerospace. Whether any of these acquisitions succeed, the point is who knows what the main business of GM will be in the year 2000?

Motorola made the same kind of strategic game change in the late 1960s. They looked at the future, and even though business was good they decided that their future did not lie in television sets and car radios. Motorola developed a ten-year plan to change their game and reinvent the company. They moved from manufacturing TVs and radios to making semiconductors and microprocessors.

American Can. As of the summer of 1986, their primary business wasn't packaging, it was financial services. They have moved to a brand-new game.

At the Pecos River Learning Center, one of the most exciting undertakings we are involved in is helping corporations make this kind of strategic move, helping them anticipate, innovate and change the game. Companies as diverse as the Lutheran Brotherhood Life Insurance Company, Du Pont, General Motors, Pillsbury and AT&T Communications have all worked with us in order to plan, refine and implement anticipatory change.

THE PERSONAL GAME CHANGE

As individual salespeople we have exactly the same challenge and opportunity as do the organizations we work for. We can wait and be shocked into change, we can keep slowly adapting behind the play, or we can make the leap. We can, as Peter Drucker strongly advises, create our own future. Anticipatory, personal strategic change—creating the future of selling instead of waiting for it to happen—is our opportunity.

It's the same process that companies use to change strategically. It starts with analyzing where our clients, markets and businesses are right now, what the trends are, where business will be in the future. Then we must ask how, as salespeople, we can best respond. Then we innovate, we invent the new game. Being out on the leading edge, inventing the new game and the new rules is where the excitement is—the excitement of discovery, of knowing no personal boundaries to what you can and cannot do.

BETWEEN TRAPEZES

A final change option. In times of great change—such as we're experiencing today—everything can seem ambiguous, and sometimes threatening. Our tendency is to hang on to what we know and not let go. Sometimes we take that to extremes. We stick our organizational heads in the sand, tell each other that nothing is really changing, and that the solution to our woes is to just go back to basics! We do this even in the face of overwhelming evidence that the entire game is changing. So here is a change strategy, a metaphor that I use and that we teach. While everything around you is changing, try to think of yourself as a trapeze artist—suspended between trapezes. We've let go of the old trapeze, the old ways of selling, and we're waiting—suspended in midair—for the new trapeze to show up. *The change paradox is that you cannot grab the new until you've let go of the old.* So our mission, in this instant of time, is to let go of the old and hang with confidence in midair, and to believe that the new trapeze will show up. And it will.

A Game Change Principle: "It makes a difference whether we consider ourselves pawns in a game whose rules we call reality or as players in a game who know that the rules are 'real' only to the extent that we have created or accepted them." *

What This Book Is All About
Summary

The changes we are experiencing right now in business and selling are so fundamental and so deep that we will not survive by just tinkering with the rules of the old game. Instead, we need to change the entire game.

THE CHANGE OPTIONS

There are three ways that organizations or individuals change:

* *Change* by Paul Watzlawick, John Weakland, and Richard Fisch.

1. *Shock:* Being shocked into change occurs when you are forced to change with seemingly no forewarning, or, as is more frequently the case, when you have ignored all kinds of predictors.
2. *Evolutionary:* A company or an individual slowly adapts to change by following the pack.

But both shock and evolution carry a high price. The cost of shock is easy to see: companies can be shocked out of existence. The cost of the evolutionary change is just as expensive over the long term: *it's the cost of lost opportunity.*

3. The third option is what game changing is all about. Anticipating the future, developing innovative responses and then strategically changing—changing the game. Creating the future.

As individual salespeople, we have the opportunity to create the future of selling by *anticipating* where our clients are going, developing *innovative* responses and then *strategically* changing—changing the game of selling. That's what the salespeople—the game changers—who are interviewed in this book are doing. They are inventing the new game of selling.

CHAPTER 2

Understanding the New Game

Our first task is understanding what our customers are going through in these turbulent economic times *and* developing the ability to see the future through their eyes. In the world of "future shock," as Alvin Toffler named it (and we are experiencing it today), it isn't enough just to stay close to your customers—the best and brightest will, in addition, be able to anticipate and prepare for where their customers are going to be in the future. The penalty for not developing that ability will be adapting by evolution. Those who travel that route will be the salespeople who follow their customers into the future, instead of moving forward with them in partnership—and they will miss being on the leading edge, where the new game is being played.

ANTICIPATING THE FUTURE

We are surrounded by confusing indicators, old industries falling by the wayside, new industries emerging. A shift from an industrial economy to an information economy. Or at least that was the prevailing wisdom a few years ago. In fact, no one really knows what's going on. In boardrooms all over the country, the same questions are being asked: What business are we really in? What business should we be in? What does the future look like? *And no one has the answers.* Organizations all across the business landscape are between trapezes, letting go of the old ways and waiting for the next trapeze to show up. What's fascinating to me is that even in the midst of all this there are patterns to how organizations —our clients—change. Patterns in how they evolve, how they grow, and how they succeed or fail. If, as salespeople, we can understand the patterns underneath the turmoil, we can, to a great extent, anticipate where business is going, where our clients are going and where we had better be going to change the game.

The Strategic Anticipation Tool

To help us here, let me introduce you to one of my heroes, business partners and close friends, George Ainsworth-Land. George wrote a book titled *Grow or Die* (not a bad motto for life in general). He is a general systems theorist. He's a pipe-smoking iconoclast who has one foot planted squarely in academia and the other in our world, business and marketing. As a general systems theorist, he is best at identifying similarities and trends that are critical to predicting the future. One of the most important models that George has created is called the Growth Model.

The growth S-curve describes how organizations and markets change. It has helped us and our clients understand and anticipate the patterns and phases of growth. With that knowledge, we have been able to better understand where our clients and our clients' clients are

The Growth Model

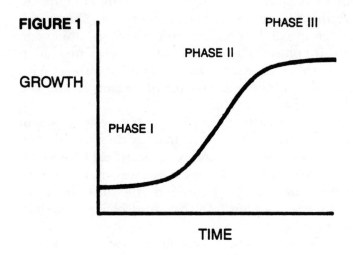

FIGURE 1

GROWTH

PHASE I

PHASE II

PHASE III

TIME

going as they confront changing market conditions and changing internal needs. The Growth Model is a strategic tool that can help us anticipate and stay close to our customers.

Survive, Succeed, Grow or Die

In George's model there are three phases of growth. Phase I is the new business, struggling to find a successful pattern—the right product or the right marketing strategy. That business either finds a successful pattern or goes out of business.

The second phase of a business—if it survives Phase I—focuses on replicating the success pattern—exploiting a niche or a market opportunity as efficiently and effectively as possible. Growth is usually rapid. Replication, "doing what we do best," and assembly-line thinking are the keys to the second phase.

But at some point late in that phase, organizations

seem to hit a wall—they've grown as much as they can grow using the old success pattern. Growth—in terms of profitability and market share—flattens out. The search for new solutions begins, and organizations attempt to enter a third phase. The call for "innovation," for changing the basic business, becomes loud and strong. With luck and skill a new success pattern emerges and the growth cycle begins again.

All organizations seem to go through these phases of growth. It's the natural way that businesses evolve. What we're seeing today, and what is critical to our strategic understanding, is that most businesses, almost our entire economy, is going through the turbulence of phase change—moving into that third phase, reinventing the business.

What's important about this model for salespeople? First, we have to avoid being "phase blind," because the phase that our customers are in is the key strategic determinator of how they respond to the marketplace—including how they respond to the salespeople who work with them. We are in a position to help the most when we see their situation *from* their situation.

If I were writing this book twenty or thirty years ago, we'd spend a lot of time trying to understand Phase I and Phase II companies—because those kinds of companies were 90 percent of our customers back then. But today that would be time and energy wasted. We're going to look just briefly at those kinds of companies, because we've been successfully selling to them for decades, so we know what they're like and how they operate.

But today most companies are going through dramatic change; they are in transition to that third phase. There's a new type of customer. And that's the customer we need to understand in detail. That customer is the future, and that's where we'll spend most of our time in this book.

Phase I: The Entrepreneur (Muddling Around Until We Get It)

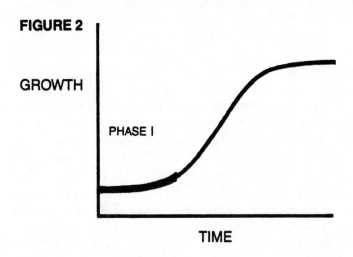

FIGURE 2

GROWTH

PHASE I

TIME

Because corporate selling is somewhat more complex than consumer selling, I'm going to use the corporate world to help explain change and the growth model. But I'll keep making connections to the individual consumer markets, because those markets are going through much the same kind of transition.

Phase I is where companies begin—and where most end. A new business comes to the market with a product or an idea, and the first demand of a business is to discover a success pattern before time runs out. The game is survival. A successful pattern might mean discovering how to produce a product cheaper or better, or discovering your "niche" in the market. Examples of Phase I companies are all around us. Every new restaurant that opens searches for that marketable difference, the perfect combination of traffic, menus and "concept."

Phase I is a lot like the old movie scenario where all three of the pilots on a 747 become incapacitated. I'm a pilot; I've flown small single-engine airplanes. I could figure out how to fly and land a 747. But the problem in this particular scenario is that the 747 would run out of fuel before I could learn how to safely land the airplane. Most Phase I companies could eventually learn how to succeed, but they run out of gas—time and money— first.

With survival as the only thing that matters, Phase I companies tend to share similar characterisitics. There is a lot of muddling around, going in one direction, then changing and moving off in a completely new direction. It's typically an exciting but stressful time, with companywide risk-taking, crisis-to-crisis management and usually a highly motivated work force.

The other important characteristic of Phase I companies—the good ones—is that they tend to be very close to their customers and to what is going on in the market. In brand-new companies, running scared and running very close to your customers come naturally. They have that visceral understanding that "being close" will make or break them. Whether they are large or small companies, they are highly responsive and usually adaptable enough to be able to move quickly when the market changes. In short, they are opportunity driven.

FLYING THE PHASE I SKIES: AIR MIDWEST

A clear example of this flexibility can be seen in the early development of Air Midwest, one of the regional airlines. As Brian Schoenthaler, the vice-president for advertising and public relations, explains, Air Midwest started by flying air ambulance and caskets in a single-engine airplane. That market dried up. They changed direction and began flying on a charter basis between cities in Kansas. They shifted again to gain contracts to fly night mail runs—whatever it took to go where the market was going. After they had developed into a regional carrier, they ordered ten new aircraft to be uti-

lized in the lucrative Texas market. About the same time, SouthWest Airlines began flying the same routes. Almost overnight, Air Midwest decided not to compete against jet service, and switched markets, moving their new fleet to New Mexico and to Midwestern routes—a sign of flexibility. All the "muddling around" finally helped them to discover a formula that led them to success in an industry that is fiercely competitive and unforgiving of even the smallest strategic mistakes. Air Midwest is now firmly entrenched as one of the most successful regional airlines.

We are awash in new Phase I businesses. Everywhere you look there are ten new companies, and nine of them are running out of gas, in the form of time or money.

Phase I ends very tangibly. Either a company fails or it discovers a successful, *replicable* pattern and moves into Phase II.

THE PHASE I ORGANIZATION

Survival oriented.
Highly entrepreneurial.
Fast movers, highly adaptable and changeable.
Perpetually cash short.
Risk-takers.

The success pattern discovered, Phase II begins with relatively fast growth. All the parts seem to come together. The product, the marketing and the timing all seem to work. The successful pattern is known, and the objective is *maximum exploitation of the pattern.* Phase I entrepreneurship is appropriately replaced by the ability to replicate. The mission now is to take the success pattern, whether a product or a marketing concept, and to duplicate it as many times as possible.

In order for a business to replicate profitably, the cor-

Phase II: The Successful Replicators

FIGURE 3

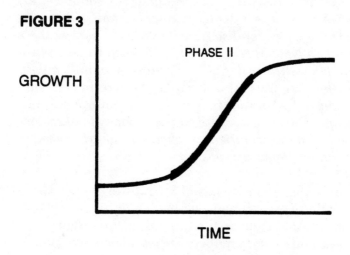

GROWTH

PHASE II

TIME

porate focus begins to shift toward producing and marketing the pattern *efficiently and effectively.* In order to accomplish the "efficient and effective" objective, Phase II companies create tight controls and boundaries. In Phase I, almost everything is permissible if it is ethical and it helps the company survive. In Phase II, innovative ideas are welcome only if they help replicate the success pattern—that is, only if they fit into the game that's being played. Rules are created to insure that the corporation remains efficient and effective.

Turning Point: Transition to Trouble

The turning point comes when the uncertainty that is so much a part of new companies gives way to a confidence about the market. Because the "pattern," be it a product or a marketing idea, has proven to be successful, the organizational focus shifts from the marketplace to internal matters. It is here that the seeds of later decline are planted—even as the Phase II company appears to be wonderfully successful. The research we did at Wilson Learning Corporation indicates that the more successful companies become, the harder it is for them to stay close to customers. That's the paradox. In fact, with certain kinds of success comes an almost inevitable drift away from the key factor that can guarantee future success: customers. In business, success seemingly breeds later failure. Unless a company is brilliantly managed and has a long-term strategic focus, one of the naturally occurring pitfalls of Phase II growth and success is a later Phase II decline, and, often, failure.

THE HORSE SPLASHES

Much of what changes the relationship between a company and its market is related to size. Without attention and effort, flexibility and market sensitivity can drastically diminish as companies reach critical mass in size and complexity.

This is very much analogous (recognizing that analogies can sometimes be treacherous) to the effect of scale in the physical world. H. F. Judson, in his book The Search For Solutions, *discusses the enormous amount of effort in science and engineering directed toward overcoming the consequences of scale. Natural forces, for example gravity, act on all things uniformly. It's the size of the body that to a large extent controls the consequences. As an illustration of this principle, Judson quotes the British biologist, J. B. S. Haldane: "You can drop a mouse down a thousand-yard mine shaft and on arriving at the bottom it gets a slight shock and walks away. A rat would probably be killed—although it can fall safely from the eleventh story of a building—a man is killed and a horse splashes."*

A bit gruesome, but it illustrates the point. Market forces—like the fall down the shaft—are basically all the same. It's the size of the body that to a great extent causes the consequences.

The small, flexible company, or a large company with small flexible work units, can respond very quickly to changes in market condition. The larger and more complex a company becomes, the less able it is to quickly adapt—to survive the fall. Finally, the large corporation that is a late Phase II dinosaur, run firmly from the top down, rigid in its rules and systems, can rarely survive the kinds of major market changes we are currently experiencing. These corporations are the splashing horses.

Nothing Fails Like Success

Two of the big sales-training clients that I had in our early days were, in retrospect, examples of the principle "Nothing fails like success." The companies were Addressograph-Multigraph and Freiden Calculators. In fact, the first $50,000 I ever received—I had the canceled check framed—came from Addressograph-Multigraph.

Both of these companies have gone through Chapter 11 bankruptcy. Addressograph-Multigraph survived, but Freiden went out of business. With the help of hindsight, the reasons are apparent. But in the 1960s it would have been hard to believe that this could happen. These companies both were product leaders in their industries and highly successful.

Addressograph-Multigraph was one of the premier companies in the offset-printing industry. As part of the research contract we had with them, I visited many of their locations, including their factory. Even then, when they were obviously successful, it was apparent when you looked hard that things were not all well. There was a lot of bureaucracy; the rules, the systems were very rigid. What was happening was very much like Alexander Hamilton's remarks about government: they were evolving toward bureaucratic convenience and authoritarian control. The organizational mentality was very much "Factory out—we make it, you sell it." Headquarters did not seem really interested in hearing what their salespeople had to say. Their focus seemed to be on reducing the production cost and the marketing cost of the product. The problem was that somewhere along the line Addressograph-Multigraph lost sight of where the industry and its customers were going. Their success at the "efficient and effective" game *blinded* them to how their market was changing, in this case to the onset of the electronic-printing revolution. Addressograph-Multigraph ended up filing for Chapter 11 bankruptcy.

The good news is that they survived reorganization and, under their new CEO, Merle Banta, and with a new name, AM International, they are slowly but positively coping with the transition from Phase II to Phase III.

Freiden Calculators was very much the same story. Freiden produced and marketed the "Cadillac" of desktop adding machines—the large adding machines with a handcrank—for the price of about $1,100. It was expensive, but a well-engineered and vital tool for accountants and actuaries. Then one day the hand-held electronic calculator showed up, priced initially at around $200, and Freiden couldn't compete. *Caught seemingly by surprise, they couldn't turn their ship around fast enough to go where the market was.* Freiden went out of business.

What drove the Freiden story home to me was that at the same time I was working with Hewlett-Packard. I remember visiting one of those small, autonomous HP plants—this one in Loveland, Colorado—and looking at one of their new prototype desktop calculators. A young Hewlett-Packard engineer told me that they could build those as small as a cigarette package. At the time their only concern was that the calculators would be so small that they would be too easy to steal.

As anyone who knows HP could have foretold, Hewlett-Packard had its eye on where the market and the technology were going. They were ready with a hand-held calculator as soon as it became feasible to market it.

What puzzled me was that Freiden, like Addressograph-Multigraph, had a bright sales force that must have seen and understood what was going on. Salespeople had to have been the first ones to see the new competition and the different products. The indicators of dramatic change were there. But somehow the message didn't get through to the home offices. Why?

Organizational Drift

The research we've done provides a glimmer of the answer to this question. Both of these companies battled what we think is one of the toughest challenges in the life of an organization: late Phase II organizational drift.

ORGANIZATIONAL DRIFT

A recent Wilson Learning research publication entitled Organizational Drift *summarizes the problem very succinctly:*

Our review of current organizational research suggests that business organizations have a strong natural tendency to drift away from their customers. In simple terms, it appears that as business organizations grow and become increasingly more complex, their "focus" gradually shifts from being primarily external to being primarily internal. Business enterprises tend to be very sensitive to the marketplace when they are in a formative stage, struggling to survive. They are attentive to the marketplace because it seems uncertain to them. In the formative stage, business organizations equate "staying close to the customer" with staying alive.

Once the equation for success is discovered, however, companies have a tendency to gradually divert their attention and resources to internal contingencies. The struggle for survival now becomes a struggle for efficiency. *The success and growth realized by the company, coupled with the considerable knowledge it has accumulated about "the business," work to dull its fear of and sensitivity to the marketplace.* The marketplace may even appear more certain than it really is to corporate leaders. *The combination of success and a preoccupation with internal matters can result in a company's isolation from the changing realities of the marketplace . . . Depending on the number of variables . . . the isolated company may find itself in deep trouble.*

Fat, Dumb and Happy: Organizational Arrogance

Look at some of your corporate clients. Do you see indicators such as increased sales but lower profits? A trend toward decreasing margins in sales or a decrease in market share? Successful price competition from smaller companies with dramatically less overhead or from small, specialized companies eating away at what often are small but profitable parts of the market?

Those are all signs of companies late in Phase II. They are about to go through phase change from Phase II to Phase III. Or they are about to die.

Other symptoms of impending shift are proliferation of corporate and administrative staff—more committees and more middle management. Too many layers of management, too many rituals and procedures can separate the leadership, the people who make strategic decisions, from the basic production workers and the salesforce, the people who really know what's going on. A

tragic example of this organizational error was what happened with the NASA Challenger disaster in January
1986. From somewhere down in both NASA and
Morton-Thiokol, a concern was raised about the effect
of cold temperatures on the rocket booster seals. Don't
launch, was the recommendation. As that message got
sent up the layers of both organizations, the message
was changed. At the top it came out, It's a beautiful day,
go ahead and launch.

Less tragically and less dramatically, the same process
occurs in organizations as they march toward phase
change. Less energy is spent on staying close to the market. Internal staffs proliferate. It seems apparent that
these were the symptoms of the disease that proved fatal
to both Addressograph-Multigraph and Freiden Calculators.

The Corporate Immune System

Because the Phase II mission is to replicate a known
success pattern, the organization has an immune system
whose task is to kill anything that doesn't fit the pattern,
anything that is thought to be out of the bounds of the
corporate success pattern. That immune system is very
pernicious. It tends to be anti-entrepreneurial, anti-
intuitive. "We need to do more studies!" is its rallying
cry. It consists of endless discouraging committee meetings where everyone's agenda is to protect his or her
turf. Finally, in the words of a very talented, motivated,
but frustrated executive of a large consumer products
firm, the immune system consists of a group of nameless,
faceless bureaucrats from *Return of the Body Snatchers*
who want everything and everybody to look the same,
and who seem to care only about numbers, cutting costs,
cutting people and improving market share.

But, you would think, how could any company em-
ploying reasonably bright, motivated people allow

what's happening in the market to go unnoticed—or go unnoticed until it's too late? The answer is, there are factors at work that are very pervasive and hard to fight, that accelerate the organizational drift.

Tom Peters and Nancy Austin, in their textbook of American business success, *Passion for Excellence*, quote a perfect illustration of how corporate perception (in this case GM's) is created, reinforced, protected—and how distant it can be from the truth. This is one of those stories that should hang over the desk of every CEO and salesperson in the country as a warning that the same process could happen to them:

He [the executive] *drives down the highway outside Detroit. All the car company employees and suppliers are virtually required to buy American cars. He looks to his left, looks to his right. "Everybody is still driving American cars" registers at some level. Then he pulls into the company garage. His car is gone over from stem to stern for the next ten hours. When he leaves work, it starts like a charm: "And the damn things do work. . . .*

If even one of the companies or even one of the car-producing divisions had moved to California, they would have learned the bitter truth: Californians just don't like American cars anymore. These odd names—Honda, Toyota, Nissan—are all over the highways out here. . . .

Late Phase II organizations tend to have the perception about their own business that "everyone is still using our product and the damn things do work." It's what they want to believe. And that is the perception that they act on, true or not—"believing is seeing." Then the prevailing corporate mentality works hard to protect the myth. It tends to force consensus and it puts enormous pressure—formally sometimes, informally all the time—on individuals or groups with dissenting opinions.

To sum up, in late Phase II an organization slowly begins to pay more attention to internal matters than to its customers. Next, under the assumption of certainty about the market, the corporation pays less and less attention to conflicting or dissenting points of view. Finally, the messengers—the bearers of bad news—are not listened to, they are not even allowed into the king's court. The stage is set.

THE PHASE II ORGANIZATION

Successful.
Focused on being efficient and effective.
Systems, rules and procedures oriented.
Management as opposed to entrepreneur oriented.

LATE PHASE II:

Lots of internal committees and studies.
Oriented toward repeating the known success patterns.
Not accepting of new or innovative ideas that are outside the success pattern.

At some point the news gets through: *The traditional business of the company cannot be the company's future business if it is to survive.* This realization is the corporation "waking up." All of a sudden the future appears to be somewhere between doubtful and disastrous. That new understanding is electric, it is *transformative.* From the boardroom to the field, nothing turns a company around faster than the visceral understanding of its vulnerability, of impending failure.

Running Awake

A company enters Phase III when it rediscovers the importance of listening to its customers and to its sales

Phase III: Grow, Change or Die

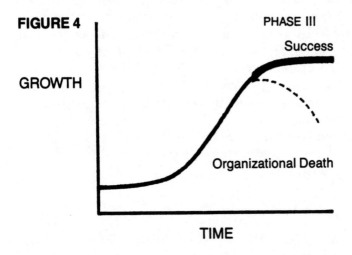

FIGURE 4

PHASE III

Success

GROWTH

Organizational Death

TIME

force. When management is uncertain about the future and the marketplace, it thirsts for information and becomes willing to open up all the channels in order to hear what's going on—the good news and *especially* the bad. Good companies create a culture that reinforces discussion, dissent and disagreement—up and down the organizational chart. As Bill Weisz, the chief executive officer of Motorola, said recently at a Wilson Learning Client conference, "The challenges today and in the foreseeable future are monumental. And while we are self-confident, we are not complacent *and we like to run very scared.*" In reality, Motorola isn't running scared—*they're running awake.* They have a culture that encourages healthy dissent, disagreement and challenge. They mandate the communication of "bad news." That culture keeps them in touch with the marketplace.

Cray Research, the leading manufacturer of supercomputers, is another example of a Phase III company. Marcelo Gumucio, the executive vice-president for marketing, echoes Bill Weisz of Motorola when he talks about the future: "We are very conscious of our competition. In our planning, we assume that the competition is going to be very tough. To be there first, we have to be lean, mean, fast and flexible—in short, concentrating on the basics. The very worst thing that we could do is become complacent. We work hard to avoid complacency by talking about the competition more than almost anything else."

"Running awake"—instead of on automatic pilot—is the first key corporate strategic process that unlocks the door to Phase III.

Innovation

The next Phase III step is innovation. Entrepreneurship and intrapreneurship are rediscovered. In fact, the reason why those are such buzz words today isn't that there are more new companies than ever before, but that so many mature companies are entering Phase III and looking for new solutions. Innovation is the only way that will happen. For a lot of organizations, that means creating new cultures and work units that experiment, take risks and make mistakes—something that the Phase II systems people and the bean counters have a hard time swallowing. (In Phase II, "To err is human; to forgive is against company policy.")

Right now CEOs of companies entering Phase III are beating the bushes looking for innovation. They may not know how to define it, but they know they need innovation and innovators in order to survive. For example, the Apple Computer Macintosh project was the essence in innovation. Apple understood that they had to innovate, to change the game in PCs, or continually lose their market share to the rest of the industry—especially IBM. Steven Jobs and his associates took a team of creative people and gave them full corporate blessing and support, and they completely reinvented the personal computer—the Macintosh. The "Mac" was the most innovative response to date to the biggest stumbling block of the personal computer: user friendliness. To my knowledge, the Macintosh is the only PC that you can purchase, take home and immediately begin using— with minimal instructions and no trauma. As customer service and responsiveness is the name of the game at IBM, so innovation is the name of the game at Apple.

Integration

Companies moving into Phase III take apart what they've learned and what they "know" and begin to look at new combinations and new ways of fitting the same parts together. They integrate the new combinations into the business.

For example, look at what GM is doing now. In Phase II it was clearly "against the rules" for them to consider a partnership with Toyota, or to write lifetime employment contracts with organized labor at the Saturn Division or to spend $2.5 billion to purchase Electronic Data Systems, or to purchase Hughes Aircraft. Those were not part of GM's Phase II world. But GM is reinventing itself. It's integrating new components into its business —components that used to be out of bounds.

Back in the mid-fifties, I was a life insurance agent for New England Life, one of the top mutual life insurance companies. It was considered sacrilege even to speculate that an insurance company—or an agent—would sell, be affiliated with, think about, or even have a good word for any investment that wasn't insurance. But even at that time, out on the fringes of the business there were agents strategically looking ahead to times of higher inflation, new competition and different market forces.

They were trying to understand other kinds of financial instruments, other products that they could integrate with insurance to provide a more complete financial solution for their clients.

Today those kinds of solutions have become the only way to thrive in the financial-services area. But such solutions would have been impossible in Phase II because formally they would have been out of bounds. Legislation kept banks, insurance companies and brokers in their separate boxes. Corporate culture did the same.

Quality

David Johns, a managing director with Federal Express Corporation, sums up their history like this: "From the beginning of the organization up until 1975 *survival* was the corporate mission. The second Federal Express unofficial paradigm was based on *speed of delivery and growth*. Today, our new corporate deity is *quality*."

That is a shift in priorities that will resonate with many companies moving into Phase III. At Wilson Learning, when we talk about quality in Phase III we are talking not only about statistical quality control or quality control personnel. We also mean what we call "Big Q" quality: a corporate culture that promotes, protects and champions quality at every level of the organization, from the board of directors to the sales force to the warehouse. "Big Q" quality permeates every aspect of Phase II companies. Quality means every individual throughout the organization being committed to doing what's right.

THE PHASE III ORGANIZATION

Running awake, very close to its customers and to its market.

Searching for innovative solutions.
Highly adaptable and changeable as the "reinventing" process goes on.
Willing to take risks.
Quality oriented, both internally and in its relationships with customers and vendors.

As companies move into Phase III, they re-acquire the visceral understanding that their business, no matter how big or formerly successful, is still vulnerable: No one is immune from the natural-selection process of the marketplace.

But not all companies will be "born again" from that understanding. There will be more companies like Addressograph-Multigraph and Freiden that will fall by the wayside or be absorbed into larger, strategically directed organizations. In fact, what we are seeing today is many of our major industries lulled asleep by their success—organizational Gullivers tied down with systems, procedures, a bias toward inaction, and boxed-in thinking that prevents them from learning and mastering the new game.

What Does Phase III Mean to Me?

As I mentioned earlier, most of our careers in selling, until very recently, were spent dealing with companies and individuals in Phases I and II. We know how to sell to those kinds of organizations and those kinds of individuals. In fact, 99 percent of sales training today still focuses on selling to Phase II companies and markets, based largely on how we sold in the past—on past knowledge and past success.

But today and for the foreseeable future, the new game is Phase III. Our clients will be running awake, looking for innovative solutions and focusing on quality. It doesn't take much imagination to understand that as more companies begin to incorporate these elements into their businesses, selling will change dramatically. I don't mean just the products that you sell, but also *how* you sell. Phase III organizations will expect a sales process steeped in innovation and quality. "Running awake," will require salespeople to respond with strategic patience, 100 percent positive intent, effort and accountability.

All these factors are changing the selling experience, changing the game in selling. Our options are to learn this new game, the rules, the roles of the participants and how the rewards are distributed, or to continue practicing our present skills and become the best players in a game that is no longer being played.

Understanding the New Game

Summary

All organizations seem to go through phases of growth. It's simply the natural way that businesses evolve. What we're seeing today, and what is critical to our strategic understanding, is that most businesses, almost our entire economy, are going through the turbulence of phase change—moving into a third phase, reinventing business.

THE PHASE I ORGANIZATION, THE NEW COMPANY, IS:

Survival oriented.
Highly entrepreneurial.
Fast mover, highly adaptable and changeable.
Perpetually cash short.
Risk taker.

THE PHASE II ORGANIZATION IS:

Successful.
Focused on being efficient and effective.
Systems, rules and procedures oriented.
Management as opposed to entrepreneur oriented.

LATE PHASE II:

Lots of committees.
Oriented toward repeating the known success patterns.
Not accepting of new or innovative ideas that are outside the success pattern.

THE PHASE III ORGANIZATION IS:

Running awake, very close to its customers and to its market.
Searching for innovative solutions.
Willing to take risks.
Highly adaptable and changeable as the "reinventing" process goes on.
Quality oriented, both internally and in its relationships with customers and vendors.

CHAPTER 3

THE RULES OF THE NEW GAME

The growth model helped us establish the big picture, and it provided the clues we needed to predict how our clients are changing. But we need to get more specific. What does the shift from Phase II to Phase III mean—specifically—to the individual salesperson? What are the new rules? From our vantage point, there seem to be six fundamental shifts, rules of the new game, that are occurring as our customers move into Phase III.

THE SIX NEW RULES

"Running awake" and more shared decision-making authority are the primary causes of the first two changes:

1. More decision-makers.
2. Longer sales cycles.

More decision-makers and longer sales cycles, in turn, make possible the next change:

3. An increase in random events.

Our clients' quest for innovation and quality is the cause of the fourth and fifth changes:

4. Demands for specific, "custom-made" solutions, instead of generic solutions (Alvin Toffler calls this "demassification").

The sixth new rule of Phase III selling is really a culmination of all the others. It concerns what our customers are really buying now and for the foreseeable future. We call this shift *"the death of the product solution."*

6. The death of the product solution.

More decision-makers and a longer sales cycle spring from the same basic cause: economic uncertainty. Anyone who has lived through the last ten years—double digit inflation, the energy crisis—knows that much of the bloom is off the economic rose. Other indicators are uncertainty about employment, business failures, mergers and now the "downsizing" of major corporations. The result is a much more cautious, intelligent buyer—one who is going to seek advice and take time to make a decision.

1. MULTIPLE DECISION-MAKERS

The first "rule change" is that there are more decision-makers involved in every major purchase. Buyers —whether inside the corporation or individual consumers—are not going to make expensive and risky decisions by themselves. They will seek advice, and attempt to spread the risk, especially for major decisions. In fact, everybody who is affected by a potential purchase will have a piece of the decision, which, loosely translated, means that more people have the ability to say no.

Add to this the trend to push authority and decision-making responsibility farther down in the organization, and you can understand why you'll need a program to identify all the players in a sales situation. The most common selling scenario in the future will not be one person sitting across the desk from a client. It will be a salesperson sitting across a conference table from three, four or more buyers or buyer influencers.

The Corporate Tower of Babel

What's important to understand is that this doesn't mean selling to four "carbon copy" buyers. For example, in the past I would sell to multiple buyers, but they would all be end-user or feasibility buyers—individuals who understood my product and who spoke the same language I did. Now as a salesperson I need to deal with people coming from fundamentally different buying motives, from different parts of the organization, and speaking different languages. Therefore, I need to speak languages different from just the language of my product. I need to speak "accounting" for the financial people, "human-resource development" for the HRD person. I need to deal with the legal beagles who think their mission in life is to stop anything that looks like a deal—good or bad. And finally, for the CEO—the ultimate buyer—I need to speak "strategic objectives." Many times I will need to bring along a "translator" or two from my organization if the client languages are too specialized.

Each of these buyers must be identified and figured out. When we talked to salespeople already dealing at this level, we found that identifying the players is an automatic beginning strategy for them. It starts with an organizational chart that represents how the client organization is supposed to work. With a little detective work, that chart is supplemented with an amended report on how things *really* work: who has the influence, how decisions are made, who is competing internally and who's cooperating, what battle scars are still fresh, what the social styles are, and so on.

Recently, a top salesperson of one of our major clients completed a sale that involved figuring out and working with twenty-seven different decision-makers, each a potential "deal killer." Because of that, the sale took over a year to complete. More buyers involved in each step of the sale complicates the process. It makes selling tougher. It requires different skills and it's a cause of the next major shift in how selling is changing.

2. LONGER SELLING CYCLES

When there are more people involved, more meetings, more presentations and more decisions, it's going to cost you in time. A major cause of the heartburn that your manager and your manager's manager feel is that none of your clients makes fast decisions anymore. Each sale is chewing up more and more corporate resources —especially time. It's expensive and it's different from how it used to be.

Twenty years ago—even ten years ago—the name of the game was how many people we could sell in the shortest period of time. As salespeople we tried *always* to compress and shorten the sales cycle as much as possible so that we could see more people. Seeing more people equaled making more money. Simple, clean, easy to understand. As a profession, we became addicted to moving from quick deal to quick deal. How many people can you see? How much business can you close in the next ten days? In this quarter?

The short-term addiction is counterproductive because it runs up against the Phase III buyer, driven by uncertainty and a desire for quality. This new buyer is going to take much more time to make a decision. He is going to look at more options, and he is going to shop around.

This hit home to me personally when we recently analyzed the change in the length of the Wilson Learning sales cycle. When I started Wilson Learning, it normally took us thirty to sixty days to close a sale with a major client. After five years, it was ninety days. The current sales force is working on sales cycles of six months to a year. That shift alone is changing our business, and the same forces are at work in your business.

The stakes are going up. The longer the sales cycle, the more rides on each sale—not just money, but prestige and careers. For example, maybe you used to make one hundred sales a year. You could afford to lose a few. Now that each sale takes longer, you have only the time and resources to make fifty or sixty sales a year. (Remember, though, your financial quota is always going up, so the fifty sales have to be much larger sales.) Each one of those sales is going to be more important. Losing one hurts more now.

No one selling in Phase III will be immune from this trend. Salespeople selling to individuals are encountering the same thing. Anytime an individual buys something that costs more than a week's wage, he is going to take more time, for a variety of reasons. The first is that same uncertainty about the economic future. Secondly, we're in a much more intelligent and sophisticated marketplace. Consumers know that they have more options than ever before. They usually know nearly as much about our products as we do. They are going to take the time to make the right decision. Buyers will not be pressured into fast decisions.

THE RETURN OF THE "BE BACK"

Some of the biggest addicts to the short-term, quick sale are automobile retail dealerships.

In that industry, there is a type of prospect that salespeople have labeled the "Be Back." That is the customer who comes in, looks around, takes some brochures, talks to the salesperson and then says, "I'll be back." In the mythology of the industry, there was no such thing as a "Be Back"—once they walked out that door, you had lost the sale. Sales training emphasized closing the sale as quickly as possible, using pressure—doing whatever was needed to keep the prospect from walking out the door without a signed order.

That's changing dramatically. Fewer individuals— mainly the very rich or the very impulsive—are going to make that kind of expensive decision on the spur of the moment. They are going to take their time, they are going to shop around. They have more options than ever before, options in terms of cars, price and the kind of salesperson they want to work with. The automotive retail sales industry, and others modeled on that industry, are reinventing their sales process—changing the game—in order not to lose the buyer who takes a couple of weeks and who might actually, in the right kind of sales situation, "be back."

The shift toward longer sales cycle impacts salespeople in two basic ways. First, simple logistics. In the Phase III market, if you have to spend more and more time on individual accounts, you're not going to be able to call on as many prospects as you might have in the past. That will dramatically affect how you are compensated. To make up for the drop in *quantity* of prospects, you will have to get more revenue from fewer *quality* prospects. (A game-changer hint: Every sale will have to be leveraged. No one will survive in business tomorrow without repeat and referral business. For more about this, see Chapter 11.)

That brings us to the second way that salespeople are affected by the shift toward longer sales cycles. Working in a long-term, multidecision sales cycle requires a different set of abilities from what we were taught when the objective was to bring in the business quickly, turn around, go out and bring in more. It will take strategic planning, patience and the ability to develop long-term personal relationships to succeed in the new game. New rules require new skills.

3. MORE RANDOM EVENTS

Longer sales cycles and more players all coming together in very turbulent times cannot help but create another factor that we are going to have to live with: It's the random event. It's the out-of-left-field, unplanned-for, hard-to-predict event.

For example, in the midst of a sale, your client's company is acquired. Or someone gets promoted—or fired. Departments are "reorganized," reporting relationships changed. Even the rumors that these events are pending can change the direction of sale—or stop it cold. All of these events are out of your control, but they can seriously alter your mental health, not to mention the bottom line.

These kinds of events have always been part of the landscape. What is new is the increasing frequency of random events. Today, one of the things that is safe to predict is that in a long sale, with multiple buyers, something unpredictable will happen. It's no longer "whether" something will happen, but "when" and "where."

Let me give you a personal example of the random event. It was the end of our fiscal year. I had been helping with a major prospect for the better part of that year. We were "calling high" in the organization, at the executive-vice-president level, and we had good connections at a variety of other levels. The Wilson Learning account manager and the regional vice-president had patiently developed the relationship and had orchestrated all our internal resources. Our advocate in the client company was the financial buyer and the executive vice-president. He shared our vision. Our proposal had been read and accepted. We all felt we had this sale made. It was in our sales forecasts, right?

So it was time for our final meeting. We brought our team to New York. Everything was moving along. They were excited. We were excited. Both client and sales teams assembled in the client's executive conference room overlooking Central Park. The executive VP started the meeting with the statement that this was the first meeting of a partnership between their company and Wilson Learning. It was only eight-thirty in the morning, and we felt that we were home free. From then until three we answered each other's questions and agreed on exactly what the outcome should be for all parties.

One thing did happen during the meeting that none of us paid much attention to at the time. The two executive VPs in our meeting had to leave for ten minutes or so to meet the new president of the operating company. We gulped, and asked, "New president?" But one of our client advocates said not to worry.

So there I was, at three-thirty in the afternoon, explaining how we would design and implement our proposal and train their people. Across from me sat their director of training. I noticed she was very quiet. We had anticipated some resistance from her. But her boss—our advocate—had told us that she would defer to him. Further, we had made what I thought was a convincing argument that she would come out a hero in all of this. I think everybody in the room believed that—except her.

As I said, she was very quiet. So I asked her if she had any questions. In a blink of an eye, she stood up, said that training was her responsibility and then swore that she would never be a part of this. So much for deferring to her boss. In retrospect, it's clear that we didn't do our job in finding out her needs, making sure that she was involved and sharing control of the proposed project. More players, more shared authority, more complexity require better strategies—you cannot shoot from the hip.

That was random event number one.

We all spent the next couple of hours strategizing on how to get her back on our side. We had a lot of good ideas and we adjourned a little shaken, but confident.

Next morning as scheduled, I had a breakfast meeting with the executive VP, our internal advocate. Our agenda was to talk about schedules. Instead, he quietly revealed to me that he had just resigned.

Random event number two.

Remember the new president? Our VP resigned because his career path—which included the presidency—had just been blocked.

So what did we do? We didn't give up. We backed up and started over again (longer sales cycles, remember?). We're rebuilding relationships with all the new players, because we believed in the opportunity—for both companies.

Turbulent times breed random events, and that is tough on everybody. We have to deal with "What's going to happen next?" as part of our day-to-day work. It's like flying. One of the cardinal rules of flying, even when everything is going smoothly, is to anticipate possible problems. In business we call this potential problem analysis. Much more of our time will be spent analyzing potential problems, playing "What if?" planning, like pilots, for every possible contingency, anticipating problems.

4. DEMASSIFICATION

Recently I had the opportunity to talk to Stan Schmitt, Du Pont's manager of development programs, one of the Pecos River Learning Center's largest and most valued clients. We were talking about what Du Pont looks for from vendors. Stan's comments spell out the trend: "We believe that we are unique. We believe that we can't really do what we have to do by buying something off the shelf. We believe that we represent a big enough market ourselves to have vendors give us what we need and shape it specifically for us."

As a buyer of goods and services, Du Pont is not interested in generic solutions. The Du Pont position is what Alvin Toffler calls "demassification": the end of the mass market. "Mass market" solutions are usually unacceptable to Phase III buyers. Part of the reason is that new commitment to quality: Everything the organization does or buys has to "fit" the quality picture, an extremely difficult stretch for many generic one-size-fits-all products. Whether they are buying financial services, computer power or consulting, buyers want *customized* products and services.

From the sales perspective, this gets to be a complicated problem. It goes like this. As a salesperson, you go out and you present your black box to a client. They say "Great, we like it, but you need to make a couple of changes inside the box so that it really fits our needs."

You take the black box back to your organization and explain the changes that need to be made. Your organization says, "You don't understand, this black box is what we sell. We don't make changes—take that message back to your client." You go back and they say, "We won't buy unless you make the changes." And so on.

The salesperson is stuck in the middle between a Phase III buyer and a company that may not understand how the business has changed. This is a scenario that is increasingly frequent as everybody searches for solutions that meet specific needs.

A good example in the consumer markets is in the financial-services area. Faced with a much more sophisticated consumer, and competition from brokers, insurance companies and even Sears, the personal banker now has to provide an integrated, customized investment plan to clients. Selling (and, yes, bankers sell) a plain vanilla savings or checking account isn't enough anymore. That's not where the profitability is for the bank, because it's not where the action is.

Sophisticated financial consumers don't want just checking accounts and loans. Rather, they want a customized, comprehensive financial plan that will help meet very specific financial goals. Don't tell them, and don't imply that they're like everyone else in their demographic group. Just like Du Pont at the corporate level, they believe that they are unique and sophisticated enough to need customized solutions.

You can begin to see how "demassification" is going to change the job of the salesperson working in a Phase III market.

5. THE SALESPERSON AS A PARTNER

The relationship between the buyer and the seller is another fundamental Phase III change. The days of the *vendor* are short-lived. The new operating principle and the goal of every salesperson working with Phase III clients is creating *long-term business partnerships.* Phase III clients are looking for partnerships that run the gamut from philosophical partner, where matching "business philosophies and cultures" is a prerequisite of doing business, all the way to financial partners—sharing the risks and the rewards on co-developed or co-marketed products.

The restructuring of the automobile supply industry —those companies that supply parts to the major automobile manufacturers—is a case in point. Detroit has gone from a traditionally adversarial relationship with its suppliers to a new Phase III relationship. In order to compete—in terms of both quality and price—in the international market, Detroit is asking its parts suppliers to be part of the team, instead of just suppliers.

When it comes to selling parts to the auto industry, there's never been much question about who's in charge. Detroit waves a stick and its suppliers jump. For years the auto makers have demanded the lowest prices around, and lately they have developed a mania for higher quality, too. But now the game has taken an interesting turn. General Motors, Ford and Chrysler want advice on everything from vehicle mechanics to car design, and to get this they're supplementing their stick with carrots.

The industry's usual one-year, multiple-source contracts, for example, are giving way to exclusive agreements that run for five years or longer. And auto companies that once revealed their requirements only a few months before parts were needed on the assembly line are now giving suppliers a headstart—sometimes years in advance. . . .

Auto makers bring in suppliers at the beginning of most product development programs and routinely

choose a single company—instead of two or three—for each part they order. The idea is to give more security to those suppliers that get the work—and also more responsibility for cutting costs and improving quality.
FROM *BUSINESS WEEK,* October 14, 1985

The auto makers are getting the message that in order for them to compete successfully, *the success of their vendors is as important as the success of the auto maker.* They are all in it together. Note that the article refers to moving from multiple vendors to a single vendor for automotive parts. You can bet that the single company is looking to a salesperson who understands partnering and the strategic picture to keep that relationship alive and healthy.

Phase III buyers are signing the big long-term contracts with partners. This trend is becoming apparent in other industries, too. The following ad, reproduced with permission from Gulfstream Corporation, is another example of the partnering interdependency. In the ad, Gulfstream is blowing their horn, but they are also blowing the horn of all their partners in the development of their new jet.

THE IBM PARTNER

A senior IBMer's description of the IBM salesperson's role:

The salesperson has to reside inside the accounts. One of our clients, from a local bank, recently said that our marketing representative knows as much about their banking operation as do most of their executives. That's what you want to achieve.

In order to help his clients achieve what they want— their competitive and strategic objectives—the salesperson has to understand his client's thinking process, how the business runs, how to get inside the company as a doer, not necessarily as a salesperson, but as a member of the organization, as a consultant. *And in many cases—this is remarkable—helping that client actually formulate his strategic objectives. Because some of the people we talk to openly tell us, "We know we could do better with computers, but the trouble is we don't have any defined strategic objectives. Can you help us define them?" To do that correctly, you forget about applications, and you forget about computers, and* you talk about what business these people are in.

What we are seeing is a major shift in perception, the blurring of the distinction of who it is that a salesperson really works for—his own organization, or his client's. Some companies understand this and reinforce it. IBM is one example. They want their salespeople to work for, and believe that they work for, their clients. Other organizations struggle against the very concept, caught in the deep-down belief that clients are adversaries, even while on the surface the organization preaches "staying close."

As the game continues to change, the role of the salesperson will be to create and nurture those long-term, mutually beneficial relationships. The pendulum is swinging from salespeople as product experts to salespeople as relationship managers. The game changers you'll meet later in this book are all relationship experts —their strength is in building and maintaining relationships.

6. THE DEATH OF THE PRODUCT SOLUTION

That brings us to the final "big picture" shift. We stepped back and asked the question, What do our cus-

It's here. Ahead of schedule.

No longer ago than March 1983, we launched the most important new airplane development program in our history.

We said we were going to design and build the Gulfstream IV.

We said it would have levels of performance and systems technology that would make it the ultimate executive jet for the balance of this century and well into the next.

We said we'd fly it in late 1985 and begin deliveries in mid-1986.

Well, we've kept our promise.

The Gulfstream IV is here. Ahead of schedule. Not just by days, but by months.

And there's simply nothing else like it.

The Gulfstream IV will fly at least 8 passengers, a crew of 3 and baggage over 5,000 statute miles non-stop in about 9 hours with NBAA IFR reserves.

Airliners can't do it any faster.

Other corporate jets can't do it at all.

The Gulfstream IV will provide this remarkab[...] productivity because everyone involved delivered w[...] they said they would deliver.

We wanted new engines for the Gulfstream IV[...] Engines that would be fuel-efficient and good neigh[...] Engines with the same high levels of dependability [...] reliability the airlines demand. Getting them called [...] massive commitment to a major engine developmen[...] program, which Rolls-Royce made.

They delivered the Tay engine. Ahead of sche[...]

We wanted the Gulfstream IV cockpit to be n[...] advanced than those in the current generation of c[...] mercial airliners. That meant designing and program[...] totally new concepts in computerized flight manag[...] systems integrated with electronic flight informatio[...] plays. It was like creating the hardware and softwar[...] the automated office of the future from scratch.

Sperry delivered. Ahead of schedule.

The Gulfstream I[...]
So advanced, it[...]

tomers really buy? We asked the customers of a lot of our clients this question. The answers we got are critical to understanding the role of the salesperson now and in the future.

To start with another perspective, let me introduce you to Wayne Townsend, manager of human-resource development for GM of Canada. GM of Canada is one of our valued clients, and Wayne is one of the experts I go to when I have questions about the automobile industry. He has a practical and strategic view of what the industry needs to be doing and where it needs to go.

Recently, Wayne was involved in a study that asked women customers what they wanted from an automobile dealership. From a whopping 80 percent, the first priority of the women interviewed was a salesperson and service manager with whom they could establish a trusting, long-term relationship. The second priority was a fair price, and the third was that they didn't want to negotiate on price—they didn't want to go through the intimidation that goes on at the closing.

This leads me to believe that in many sales situations, in many industries, salespeople and customers are digging two tunnels instead of one: *Salespeople are selling products and customers are buying relationships.*

It's clear that the product distinction—comparing your black box to your competitor's black box—is becoming the least important part of selling. The time-tested strategy of comparing product features is becoming a dead-end strategy. And it's a strategy that's very easy to beat. Think about your industry, specifically your company's products and your competition's products. No matter where you look, what you see are entire industries developing products in lock step, so that now *most products in almost every industry appear indistinguishable from one company to another.* Don't let that statement ruffle your company-loyalty feathers. Sure, there may be product differences, but these are seldom evident to the customer. Those differences are not what customers or clients usually look for.

A senior executive for IBM puts it this way:

The gigantic differences between products are getting to be very difficult to find. We're talking about inches now, millimeters. . . . There are some parts [of our products] that have a big advantage over the competition. But there are some places where we are at a loss. But the point is that the client doesn't care anymore. If we want to do something in a millionth of a second versus a trillionth of a second, who cares? The client doesn't listen to that anymore. The only people that listen to that even a little bit are the Japanese clients. They like the technical part of the problem. But even then, as in other places, it's the application that counts. The client wants results—he wants to grow by 5 percent. He doesn't care whether he does it with a piano or a dishwasher or a computer. He wants to grow. Now, how is he going to grow? Are you going to help him grow? If you are, you're the guy he wants to talk to. And if you're selling computers, fine. It doesn't make any difference.

Whether you are selling cars, telephone systems or payroll software, at the feature, benefit and price level *most products look alike.* Selling product is a dead-end strategy. It isn't what clients are buying. Wayne Townsend commented that one of the prevailing beliefs at the auto-dealership level is that if GM would just develop a world-class car, their problems would be over. As Wayne says, while product quality is vital, it's not the whole answer, because buyers are looking for more.

WHAT PHASE III BUYERS ARE *REALLY* BUYING

What most buyers want is three things:

1. *An Adequate Solution.* Not to be confused with an inferior solution or a barely suitable solution. It means one that solves the problem as promised. This is a departure for many of us who grew up on and were nurtured by the legend of product leadership. But the truth is that maintaining product leadership, at any company, in any industry, is impossible. IBM can't do it, GM can't do it, Prudential can't do it. *And that is appropriate and acceptable* because clients are not buying product leadership. These companies understand that. But if that isn't what clients are buying, what are they buying?

2. *A Trusted Consultant.* A salesperson and company they can trust: that's what clients are buying. Faced with no discernible difference in products, what buyers are looking for are salespeople who have their clients' interests at heart. More than ever before, buyers are looking for salespeople who are consultants, whose primary task is to help the buyer make the best decision possible from a myriad of choices.

A close friend of mine, Newton Long, is one of the "whiz kids" in the automotive industry. His mission is to bring the dealerships into the future of selling. A while ago, Newton was working with a Sacramento dealership. He made a bet with the dealer. Newton said that he would spend a couple of weeks as a salesperson. He would do it with virtually no product knowledge. His focus would be completely on establishing a trusting relationship with his prospects. He would tell the prospects up front that he didn't have all the answers— but that he knew where to get them. The bet was that Newton could sell more cars than the average for a salesperson in that dealership. Newton won the bet. Buyers are looking for salespeople they can trust. They are looking for consultants who are on their side.

3. *Value-added Service.* The third element that buyers are seeking is value-added service. "Value added" is probably one of the most beat-up, often quoted, *misunderstood* phrases in selling today. In 1965, when Wilson Learning coined the sales definition of "value added," we defined it as exceeding the expectations of the client. It means getting outside the role of "salesperson" in order to solve the customer's problem. That idea changed the way a lot of people sold. The dilemma is that every time a salesperson exceeded a client's expectation, that *became an expectation* of the client, so that the next time it no longer was "valued added." We have increased the expectations of our clients. Now salespeople have to keep up.

Exceeding expectations by getting outside the boundaries of the job description is a vital theme in this book. We're going to look at how to do it in a variety of ways —and we'll come back to "value added" in detail, because it's a very important part of the future of selling.

Adequate solution, trusted consultant salesperson, value-added service—if I were you, I'd be saying, "This all sounds good in theory, but who has built a successful marketing strategy on this principle?"

Recently I was speaking to an executive round table of a large electronics firm. I had just finished explaining adequate solution, trusted salesperson and value-added service. The marketing VP challenged me on this point. He asked me to give one example of a company that ever made it with only an adequate product solution. (Remember, I said adequate, not inferior.) I answered, "IBM."

He stood there for a minute. It sank in. He was stunned. Then he turned to his peers and told them that they had done it to themselves. He said, "We've convinced our sales force that year after year we are going to have the very best product. And the fact of the matter is that we haven't been able to do it. We've disillusioned our people, and they are leaving. Had we put emphasis on trust and value-added service, we wouldn't be in this kind of trouble."

That was a powerful session. But think about how IBM works. They have never been the breakthrough technological company. Peter Drucker calls IBM the "world's foremost creative imitator." What IBM understands, better than any other major organization, is what their customers really want. They have built their reputation with products that solve the problem, followed by a reputation for one of the most trusted sales forces in the world and, finally, a dedication to service. Customers know that IBM will be there if there is a problem with any of their equipment.

IN A NUTSHELL

The story of the shift from Phase II to Phase III is really this: where it was once simple, it's now complex. Where I used to sit across the table from just one client, now there are teams of people on both sides of the table, and *I* am on both teams. And the process seems to take forever. Where I used to sell one or two kinds of black boxes, now we are being asked to *change what's in the box* to meet specific needs. If this isn't different enough, I know that the careful plan that I've created will be changed at some point by events that I can't even predict. On top of all that, clients want innovation and quality, and they are looking for long-term partners. In a nutshell, that's the future of selling.

A CASE IN POINT: MOORE BUSINESS FORMS
AND SYSTEMS DIVISION

An example to summarize the changes in selling. The Business Forms and Systems Division of Moore is one of our oldest and best clients. Gary Hultgren, an associate director of marketing, has been instrumental in helping us understand the Moore world and how it's changing. The changes the Moore sales force is going through are virtually identical to the changes that most of us in selling will experience.

For over a hundred years the Business Forms and Systems Division has produced and marketed business communication products, the forms and paper products that we use daily. For example, next time you get a traffic ticket, look down in the corner of the ticket and in small print it will probably say "Moore."

But at Moore, it's a business that's being strategically managed through dramatic change.

And nowhere is the change more dramatic than in the sales force.

For a hundred years, Moore salespeople sold product —printed business forms. They typically dealt with comptrollers, purchasing agents and the like, and it frequently was a sale against price competition.

Today, Moore is in transition from a communications-product company to an information-management company, selling information-management systems— an entirely new game for the Moore sales force. Instead of only having to know business forms, design, prices and how to construct custom forms, now a Moore salesperson needs to be able to analyze how information is managed in a company and must be able to present all sorts of high-tech—including electronic—information-management solutions. The salespeople still sell forms, but now as part of a comprehensive information-management system.

How has this changed the game for Moore sales-people?

More People, Higher Up. First, the sale takes place at a higher level in client organizations. They have to call on the individuals in the organization who have the total view. That means calling at the CEO, VP and director levels.

Longer Sales. A Moore salesperson used to call on a couple of clients every morning, talk about product, talk about price and move on. In a systems sale, weeks can be spent in just problem analysis, and even more time in developing and presenting and reviewing solutions—an entirely new game requiring much more strategic patience.

Team Selling. Moore salespeople now work with system analysts, designers and consultants, leading a team of experts for Moore and from the client company—in a problem-solving partnership.

Time Management. How the Moore salespeople spend their time has changed dramatically. Much more time is spent planning and strategizing—almost 75 percent —much less time is spent in front of the customer. And as Gary Hultgren will tell you, to a lot of experienced Moore salespeople that feels wrong.

Moore Business Forms and Systems Division is asking the sales force to make dramatic changes. Knowing the Moore organization, I know they'll be successful. They understand their new business, they understand that it doesn't happen overnight; that it takes time, support and resources. But they also understand that the opportunity window opens and shuts quickly. Moore Business Forms has made the leap—made a commitment to the new game and to helping their salespeople learn the new game.

FROM OBOIST TO CONDUCTOR

Imagine the difference between someone who plays an instrument in the orchestra and the orchestra conductor. That's the degree of change we're talking about. A jump in magnitude to different skills, different responsibilities and new ways of thinking. The oboe player will give way to the orchestra conductor who *manages* the sales process, the relationship, the resources and *leads* teams of players from both sides. Conductors know how they want something to turn out—how the symphony should sound—and they know how to lead the orchestra to create music where before there was only a collection of sounds. The orchestra conductor is the metaphor for the new salesperson. Phase III selling will be more complex, more sophisticated, involving a higher order of skills. But if you decide to play this game, it will be more rewarding, more fulfilling and a lot more fun.

The Rules of the New Game
Summary

There are six fundamental shifts in selling that are occurring as our customers move into Phase III.

1. There are more decision-makers.
2. Sales cycles are longer, eating up much more of the salesperson's time.
3. With more people involved in every sale, taking place over a longer period of time, all occurring during the turbulence of phase change, there will be more random events that can significantly alter the direction of a sale.

4. Clients are demanding specific, "custom-made" solutions, instead of generic solutions—i.e., "demassification."
5. Clients are looking for partners instead of just vendors. Successful salespeople are working on developing much longer-term, mutually beneficial relationships.
6. The last rule change, "the death of the product solution," is really a culmination of all the others. It concerns what clients are really buying:

An adequate solution—not to be confused with an inferior solution or a barely suitable solution. It means one that solves the problem as promised.

Consultants—that is, salespeople they can trust.

Value-added service—exceeding customer expectations.

CHAPTER 4

THE GAME CHANGERS

There is a group of salespeople who are responding creatively to the changes in selling that we've discussed. They anticipated many of the changes and developed responsive selling solutions in order to meet the present and future needs of their clients. We call them the game changers, and in large part they are responsible for the new game in selling.

In order to understand how game changers get to the point where they become the masters of the game instead of pawns in the game, let's step back and trace how professional salespeople develop.

THE ROAD TO SUCCESS

For a number of years, we have been researching how salespeople grow and how they become successful. Our first "Aha!" was understanding that selling is a developmental process. No matter what many companies and sales managers believe, it takes time, experience (including mistakes) and lots of learning to become a professional salesperson. Especially to get to the top of the profession. That sounds simple enough, but the reality is that even today, in many industries, new salespeople are thrown out on the street far too quickly: if they survive, that's great, if they don't they should try another career.

Today, as salespeople move from being just players in the orchestra to being orchestra leaders, that model won't work. *Orchestra leaders are developed.* Most of our major clients understand this and they are working on developing their salespeople, putting in place entire curriculums to support learning throughout a salesperson's career. That's the direction that all industries and most companies are going to have to follow in order to develop salespeople who can respond and succeed in an increasingly complex and competitive marketplace.

THE THREE PHASES OF GROWTH

Just as selling itself has gone through three phases of growth and changes, so too have salespeople undergone three phases of growth. In each phase salespeople seem to have different needs, expectations and ways of working. As we did for our clients, we'll move through the first two phases quickly and concentrate on Phase III salespeople, the game changers, because it's those salespeople who are reinventing selling.

THE JOURNEY

If you've been in selling for a while, you've experienced much of what you're about to read. As we grow in selling, we do things differently. The "how to" part of

FIGURE 5

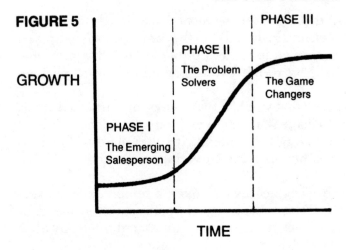

GROWTH

PHASE III

PHASE II
The Problem
Solvers

The Game
Changers

PHASE I
The Emerging
Salesperson

TIME

selling, and our beliefs about selling and about our
clients continue to change as we develop.

The Phase I Salesperson: Survival

Phase I salespeople are motivated by a most basic
need: survival. This is your first sales job, or your first
year with a new company. You don't know what to do,
what to say or really what selling is all about. You're
dealing with everything from the next call to whether
selling is the right profession. Phase I is a period of great
dependency. Ideally, there is an "umbilical cord" between you and your sales manager. Phase I salespeople
require role models, total safety and strong support until
they learn how it's done. They depend on their sales
manager for answers, protection and guidance.

Think back to your first year or so of selling. If you
were anything like me, you wanted to be told what to
say to a prospect. Your attention was on what was going
on inside you, and your fear was about doing or saying
the wrong thing in front of a prospect. You lived and

died by the call. You were not necessarily concerned with meeting the needs of the prospect. Usually you were so relieved to make it through those first presentations that you didn't even hear how the prospect responded.

You knew that you had two weeks, or thirty days or six months to make it, to begin making your quota or at least to begin paying for yourself. It's very hard to focus on anything other than on surviving under those circumstances.

Let me introduce Don Walker, a senior account executive for Wilson Learning Corporation. Don's experiences as a Phase I salesperson are something many of us have shared. He says:

I started selling with Procter and Gamble in 1965. For my sales training, I met an experienced salesperson —he had been selling for two years—at the Holiday Inn outside Baltimore, and he spent a week with me showing me the ropes. He'd make a sales presentation one day and then I would repeat it the next. After a week he went home, and I never saw him again—that was my initial sales training.

That first phase was tough, a lot of fear, lack of confidence—the proverbial salesperson who hates to get out of bed in the morning. It was go out and survive. Do the best you can—and we'll see how it works out.

My own first year of selling insurance was a classic example of evolving through Phase I. Prospecting amounted to trying to find people who fit *my* presentation. I made a lot of cold calls, I went through dozens of different selling approaches. I memorized my lines— the problem was that many of my prospects didn't know theirs. My goal was always simple: to make my monthly draw by hook or by crook and thus survive in the business. My focus was inward. Questions kept popping up in my brain, like "How does this affect me?" "What will happen if I don't make this sale?" "How can I get through next week?"

At some point, I had a glimmer that there was a better way. It sounds very simple now, but then, as a twenty-four-year-old struggling life insurance agent, it was a major revelation. First, as a new agent I had been told what to do and what to say. I was told that success would be mine if I *never* deviated. After a few months the lights went on. I found out that everybody deviated; no one who was successful was using the memorized, company-approved sales talk. They all had started that way, but they became successful when they began to do it their own way. It was the only way to succeed.

So I began to explore what was actually going on, and I realized that I was doing everything backward. Instead of trying to find prospects who fit my presentation, what I needed to do was to fit my presentation to the prospects I found. A simple idea, but it changed selling for me. I began to actually make sales. And very importantly, my beliefs changed: I began to believe that I was going to make it. That made all the difference.

A New Pair of Glasses

Once you move from believing that failure lurks behind every corner to knowing that you're successful and you're going to make it, you begin to see everything differently. And seeing everything differently changes what you do and how you think. It's like a new pair of glasses. Once you've seen the difference they can make, you never go back to the old ones.

Think about the time when you first realized that you were going to succeed. How it changed everything. It changed your relationship to your work, to your clients, your manager and, importantly, the relationship you had with yourself. That feeling that "things are different" is an important part of the phase change experience, and we'll experience it again in greater magnitude in the shift from Phase II to Phase III.

THE PHASE I SALESPERSON

Survival oriented.

Inwardly focused (How does this affect me? Am I going to make it?).

Wants to be told what to say and do—highly dependent on the sales manager.

Views clients as adversaries, selling as competition.

Works at managing a sales call.

Phase II Salespeople: The Problem Solvers

The Phase II salesperson strongly resembles the Phase II company: A success pattern is developed, perfected and replicated—salespeople hit their stride, begin making or exceeding quota. After what seems like months of just barely making it, they have that sudden realization that they "get" the business, it becomes familiar and predictable. Phase II salespeople know all the rules, and all the ins and outs of the whole system.

As they become experts, they move from dependency to being independent. They rely more on their own sense of the market and their own judgment. They are comfortable changing and adapting a sales process to meet the needs of a prospect. They are good at face-to-face selling.

The Phase II salesperson is a problem solver. Show him a problem that fits within his toolbox of solutions, and he has the answers, the sales process, the right "black box" and the contract all ready to go.

Phase II salespeople are very tactically oriented.

Rules, product specifications and price competition are the domain of the Phase II salesperson.

As success comes to the Phase II salesperson, so does reinforcement. Self-esteem needs are met. Successful salespeople are compenstated well—and they should be. If the organization is savvy, successful salespeople are put on pedestals as corporate heroes. They are looked to for advice, asked to help train and mentor new salespeople. The move up in the organization. The Phase II salesperson is the standard-bearer today. The majority of successful salespeople are problem solvers and they are good at it. They are the experts in that game.

Unfortunately, that game is changing.

THE PHASE II SALESPERSON

Success oriented.
Problem solvers.
Good at tactical selling.
Product experts.
Independent.
Good at managing a multiple-call sales process.

The "Never Enough" Game

A story and a model to illustrate what typically happens next to successful salespeople—and what begins the transition to Phase III. A few years back at Wilson Learning we did a film for the insurance industry called "Ten Like Me." In the film, we interviewed ten of the top second-year insurance salespeople from across the country. These people were already big hitters and close to the top of their profession. I had them all over for dinner after the taping. After about an hour of loosening up and general talk about the industry, I asked them how they all felt. They all said they felt great. Then I asked, "Really—how do you feel?" Silence. Then it poured out. These people were terrified. They felt under enormous pressure to succeed, to be better than they had been the previous year. (During that evening I could feel that some of them were thinking, I shouldn't be eating dinner, I should be making phone calls!) They felt that they were losing the contest of chasing the rabbit—it kept getting farther and farther away the faster they chased it. The consensus of the group was that they would have to work even harder just to stay in place. Not a very fulfilling prospect.

They were involved in a game called "never enough." The rule of the game is simple: No matter how successful I become, no matter how many rewards, toys and other trophies I collect, it never feels like enough. I never feel fulfilled, I never feel as if my life and work have meaning. The "never enough" game can never be won. But it is also the dominant game being played in business today.

Beyond Success

Now the model. Around the same time that I had dinner for the insurance salespeople, I was speaking at a meeting of the International Young Presidents Organization in Vienna. There were twenty other faculty members addressing around a thousand members of this prestigious group. It wasn't until I got there that I discovered that a VIP in my life was also on the faculty, Dr. Victor Frankl. Dr. Frankl had written a powerful book called *Man's Search for Meaning* about his experiences as a prisoner in the Nazi concentration camps. That book had been a major turning point in my early career. I was very excited to meet him face to face. At the time he was seventy-six years "young" and had just started flying lessons. He was one of those people who challenge your concepts of what you can and cannot do.

What he shared with that group in Vienna helps explain the "never enough" game that the ten top second-year salespeople were playing and also what goes on inside a lot of highly successful salespeople as they struggle between apparent success and a growing sense of frustration.

Dr. Frankl drew a line he called the failure–success line:

Failure _____ Success

He told us that we usually get a lot of reinforcement on how we're doing on this line. Most of us strive to stay on the right side of this continuum, the success side. When we finally make it over there, or have been there for a while, we expect feelings of great accomplishment. We have become the successful person that our parents hoped for and that we dreamed about. We expect manna to flow directly to us from heaven because we've made it!

But of course it never happens. We seldom get the feelings that we believed would accompany success. Even when everything King Midas touched turn to gold, it still didn't make him happy.

Instead, we sometimes feel frustrated, or, like the new insurance agents, we just keep trying harder, as if that dimension—the "never enough" game of success—is the only game that we are allowed to play.

But Frankl saw a much larger picture and larger potential for all of us. He said that we are not living only on a failure–success continuum. Although being successful is important, it's only part of the whole human being. He then drew another line, intersecting the first. This he called the fulfillment–depression line:

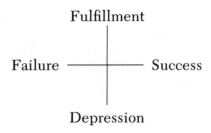

Frankl said that if we all got together and talked about it, we'd probably all agree that life was about both success and fulfillment—the upper right-hand corner.

He went on to say that we all knew people who were successful and yet depressed. And everybody in that room could understand the lower left-hand corner, being depressed and being a failure. But the Young Presidents—each one a highly motivated, highly successful individual—struggled with the idea that someone could be a "failure" and yet be fulfilled. To make that point, Frankl read three letters from three different individuals who shared one thing in common—they were in prisons, on Death Row. A position that would have to put you on the left side of the success–failure line. But each of these letters was the testament of a human being who had found a powerful source of fulfillment in his life, in very difficult circumstances. My guess was that many in that hall would have given up some of their time on this planet to experience the degree of fulfillment that was coming through in those letters.

Frankl helped us understand that success and fulfillment are independent of each other. Successful individuals need to integrate entirely new dimensions into their lives in order to keep growing as human beings.

This session with Victor Frankl impressed me so much that we changed the mission statement of Wilson Learning. It had been "Helping people and organizations become as much as they can be." To that we added "Performance with fulfillment." We wanted to help individuals—or assist their organizations in helping them —live and work in the upper right-hand quadrant.

THE KEY TO PHASE III: THE SEARCH FOR FULFILLMENT

The fulfillment that Dr. Frankl spoke about proved to be the key to Phase III salespeople. When we interviewed them it was obvious that they were very successful, but there was also something else about them. You couldn't touch it, measure it, or videotape it, but you knew right away by meeting and talking to them that they seemed plugged into an entirely different game than the rest of us. High-level performance was only one element of what these people were about. When we dug a little deeper, when we got into things that were not just about selling, we discovered the missing element: high-level fulfillment. Phase III salespeople live, and strive to live, in the upper right-hand quadrant. Fulfillment—who they are—is just as important as what they do.

The Nine Dots

To get a sense of the kind of change brought about by this powerful combination, I'm going to use an old but vivid exercise. We've used it at Wilson Learning for twenty years to encourage creative, innovative thinking.

The instructions are to connect all nine dots with four straight lines—without lifting your pencil from the paper. Try it out on some scratch paper.

There are two ways to attack this problem. The first is trying all sorts of combinations of lines inside the nine

FIGURE 6 A

•   •   •

•   •   •

•   •   •

dots. That's the conventional way. It's like the solution that the ten insurance agents were thinking of—"If I only work a little harder, make more money, I'll get the feelings I want." Trying to solve the puzzle by working inside the nine dots, with conventional solutions, won't work.

The solution to the puzzle is to get outside the nine dots, to expand your frame of reference. See p. 90 for the solution to the puzzle.

Changing the Game: Getting Outside the Nine Dots

Getting outside of the nine dots is the metaphor for the kind of change that occurs to salespeople to move them into Phase III. Successful salespeople come to the conclusion that work isn't solely about the success–failure continuum. They decide that they are here to do important things—things other than just be successful. This is a turning point in many people's lives.

It's quitting the "never enough" game—letting go of all those rules that dictate what you can and cannot do.

Instead of being a rule follower, you become, for your life and your work, a rule maker. It's the difference between being the master of the game and being a pawn in the game. Once you change your way of thinking and experience the fulfillment of being a game changer instead of a game player, of being in charge, you can never go back to the old way of doing things.

Selling Outside the Nine Dots

How this kind of change affects selling is what Part II of the book will explore. But let's preview some of the major shifts that really declare the difference between Phase II and Phase III salespeople.

WHY THEY WORK

The first shift is in the internal game—*why* Phase III salespeople work. Although money and success are important, Phase III salespeople typically aren't motivated by money.

One of the things that ANN SPINAZZOLA of North-Western Mutual Life will tell you is that money might be how we keep score—but it isn't why she works:

I think that when people are just after the money it will never work. Now, they might make a lot of money initially, but they'll never really be happy. Or successful. It's a principle that really comes out of the Bible. If you are after it for your own will, your own self-centered ego, your wealth and power, it's never going to work.

Phase III salespeople work to express themselves, not to prove who they are.

Because of that shift, Phase III is, to a large part, about quality. When you ask yourself every morning, "How

FIGURE 6 B

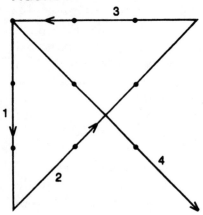

can I best express who I am?" instead of "How can I make this sale?," the answers you find go much deeper. As you'll see, there are recurring themes of integrity, honesty, effort, courage and accountability.

Read what MIKE WILHELM, a sales manager for Cray Research, has to say about Phase III salespeople:

The integrity of the Phase III salespeople is of the greatest importance to them. They wouldn't push a point to get an advantage. They'd rather take it on the chin, because credibility is so much a part of them. Not just as salespeople, but as human beings. They're comfortable with themselves, they don't get concerned over setbacks. They've mastered their professions, they're relaxed in their roles.

THERE IS NO SUCH THING AS FAILURE

The next significant shift is that game changers don't believe in failure. It's almost as if they don't exist on that failure–success line. They see work—and their lives—as a series of learning experiences. They rarely use the word "failure." Not worrying about failing, not being disabled by fear of failure, allows them to try new things, to experiment and stretch the definitions of the jobs.

OUTWARD FOCUS

Phase III salespeople, when they are at their best, are completely outwardly focused. Their purpose in selling, as we'll see, is to serve their clients. They eat, sleep, live and reaffirm that purpose daily. They almost always are on the side of their clients, anticipating their needs, making sure that their clients get what they want. It's a very powerful position.

CREATIVE

Game changers see selling as a creative experience. They see themselves as creative individuals. They don't want to do the same thing over and over again. They want to create, innovate, to be continually changing the game—to leave their mark. Whether it's in developing a new product or new service combinations or new relationships with clients, they want always to stay outside the nine dots.

STRATEGIC THINKERS

Phase III salespeople play at the strategic level. They are looking for the big opportunities. They are comfortable speaking about strategic, long-term needs with clients. They are comfortable dealing at very high, strategic levels in their client organizations.

In the greater sense, I don't like to focus in on the direct sale. I expect the direct sale. My job is to corral all those strategic things that come in. I can't get all that client's business and I can't get all their growth if

I don't understand the larger picture. If you understand the larger, strategic picture, all the rest will follow.
                                   ERIC CARLSON, Du Pont

RELATIONSHIPS

A very significant difference between Phase III salespeople and others lies in how they view the relationships they have with clients. Phase I salespeople see clients as adversaries. Phase II see clients as business acquaintances. Phase III people work best with partners and friends. Those are the kinds of relationships they try to establish.

I have a client who is a close friend of ours. The first sale I made to him was a term policy to cover a loan at a bank—maybe a four-hundred-dollar premium. This guy bought the policy, moved into a new building. He had called me up one day and said "I'd like some help, I need a mortgage." I didn't know anything about mortgages in those days, but eventually I got him in touch with somebody who did give him a loan that enabled him to move into that building. The mortgage brokers wanted to pay me a fee, but I'm not in the brokerage business or the real-estate business. I did something for my friend because that's what I believe my job is.
                    LARRY MANN, Aetna Life and Casualty

TEAM PLAYERS AND LEADERS

The Phase III salespeople we've gotten to know are leaders. But leaders in the true spirit of leadership— they're team players. They've gotten their egos out of the way; they understand that their success belongs to their team. They work hard for their team.

THE NEW GAME PLAYERS

These are the basic characteristics of Phase III salespeople, how they view their work and their clients. It's clear that they are playing a game different from conventional wisdom. By getting outside of conventional wisdom, outside of the nine dots, by plan, luck, accident and design, Phase III salespeople have anticipated where their clients are going and have developed innovative solutions and changed the game.

The game that Phase III salespeople have changed to is the new game of selling.

The Game Changers

Summary

Salespeople develop through three phases. Just like organizations, in each phase salespeople seem to have different needs, expectations and ways of working.

THE PHASE I SALESPERSON:

Survival Oriented.
Inwardly focused (How does this affect me? Am I going to make it?).
Wants to be told what to say and do—highly dependent on manager.
Views clients as adversaries, selling as competition.
Works at managing a sales call.

THE PHASE II SALESPERSON:

Success oriented.
Problem solver.
Good at tactical selling.
Product expert.
Independent.
Good at managing a multiple-call sales process.

Phase III is about high-level performance *and* high-level fulfillment.

Integrating success and fulfillment into life changes how salespeople think and sell in Phase III.

THE PHASE III SALESPERSON:

Works for fulfillment as well as success.
Doesn't believe in failure.
Outwardly focused.
Creative.
Strategic thinker.
Develops long-term friendships with his clients.
Team player and leader.

PART II

WINNING THE NEW GAME OF SELLING

SIGN POST

Let's stop here and connect the three major themes of the first part of this journey before we move on.

Clients Moving to Phase III

First, most of our clients—organizations and markets—are moving to Phase III. What that means is that more clients are "running awake," searching for innovation and quality, and pushing more authority down the organizational chart.

The New Rules of Selling

Secondly, the shift to Phase III is changing how we sell to these clients in the following ways:

Longer sales cycles.
Multiple buyers and decision-makers.
An increase in random events.
Demassification (an increase in the requests for customized products and services).
The "product solution" is no longer what clients are buying.

The Game Changers

The final theme is the emergence of Phase III salespeople—game changers, the individuals who are walking away from the old game of selling and inventing the new game in order to meet the needs of Phase III clients and meet their own needs for fulfillment.

PHASE III THINKING:
THE STRATEGIC THOUGHT PROCESSES

In the previous chapter I said that what set Phase III salespeople apart was how they think, rather than what they did, said or sold. In Part II of this book, we're going to look at seven specific ways of thinking called Strategic Thought Processes. Some of the STPs are shared by most Phase III salespeople, others are shared by just a few. But all seven STPs are outside the nine-dots ways of thinking about our selling, our clients and ourselves.

The first two Strategic Thought Processes are about the internal game:

STP No. 1: You cannot fail.
STP No. 2: Selling on purpose: helping others get what they want.

Next, we'll look at the creative part of selling:

STP No. 3: Creating the future.

Finally, we'll explore innovative and original thinking in the selling relationship, and in the business of selling:

STP No. 4: Partnering.
STP No. 5: Leading the team.
STP No. 6: Value added.
STP No. 7: Applying the principle of leverage.

NINE GAME CHANGERS

Before we begin our exploration of the Strategic Thought Processes, let me formally introduce to you nine salespeople—game changers—who will act as our guides to the STPs. They come from a variety of industries. They are four women and five men. They range in experience from five years of selling to over twenty.

What connects them is how successful they are and how they think about their customers, about selling and about themselves. They will help explain and illustrate the thinking differences that are the hallmarks of Phase III salespeople.

The Game Changers:

LARRY MANN, Aetna Life and Casualty, Los Angeles, California.
For seven years, Larry has been the top producer for Aetna Life and Casualty, for twenty-five years a member of the Aetna Leader's Club, a yearly award to the top two hundred Aetna salespeople.

DIANE FLIS, Tamaroff Buick, Detroit, Michigan.
Diane has been a member of the Buick Sales Masters since 1979. She is one of the most successful automobile salespeople in the country, averaging yearly sales 250 percent over the average. Diane sells, on average, one car every day.

CHARLES BRECKENRIDGE, Cray Research, Pleasanton, California.
Chuck Breckenridge has been in the computer industry for over twenty-five years, as an engineer and a salesperson. He has sold more supercomputers than anyone else in the world. Out of the seven American supercomputers that have currently been produced, Chuck has sold or installed the first machine for six out of the seven. His total sales volume is upward of $400 million and he averages three sales a year compared with an

industry average of one machine every one and a half years.

ALAN BRASLOW, Five Technologies, Woodcliff, New Jersey.
Five Technologies is a leader in the human-resources-systems industry. Alan's personal production is in excess of $2 million annually—in an industry where $500,000 in sales is considered successful.

ERIC CARLSON, Du Pont Automotive Development Center, Troy, Michigan.
Eric has been with Du Pont for thirteen years, nine of them in sales of polymer products to suppliers of the automotive industry. He is one of the most successful Du Pont polymer salespeople in a very difficult market. In his first territory, he went from $2 million in 1976 to $5 million in 1980 to $10 million in 1984—all at a time when the U.S. automotive industry was going through a serious slump. Typical of a strategic salesperson, Eric devised and executed a strategy that increased Du Pont's market share from 10 percent to 70 percent in two years.

KATHY MONTHEI, Delta Dental Plan of California, Oakland, California.
Kathy is Delta Dental Plan's top producer. Success in her business is around $1 million in sales annually. In Kathy's first seven years, she has sold $12 million. In addition, none of the companies she has sold to has ever terminated Delta Dental Plan of California.

ANN SPINAZZOLA, NorthWestern Mutual Life, Dallas, Texas.
Ann and her husband run their own agency in Dallas. Ann left teaching high school to become a life insurance

salesperson. She is now the top saleswoman for NorthWestern Mutual. In her seventh year of business she did $40 million in life and disability insurance.

EILEEN TERTOCHA, Skipper Morrison Realtors, Atlanta, Georgia.
Eileen has been the "Salesperson of the Year" for ten consecutive years with Skipper Morrison Realtors. She has an annual sales volume of over $9 million.

DON WALKER, Wilson Learning Corporation, Columbia, Maryland.
For the lion's share of his eight years with Wilson Learning Corporation, Don has managed only one account. He has developed that account from a single training seminar in 1977 to a $2.5 million annual account in 1986. He has averaged a million dollars in sales between 1984 and 1986.

Although there will be other voices—salespeople, sales managers, and the like—these nine will be our guides to the thinking that is Phase III, the thinking that is changing the game in selling.

CHAPTER 5

STP NO. 1:
YOU CANNOT FAIL

This Strategic Thought Process is the foundation. It's an ability that most game changers share, one that helps them to keep growing and learning while the business of selling becomes a higher-stakes, more complex and more competitive game. Game changers have developed personal strategies which allow them not to be stopped by obstacles that would paralyze many people, and which help them to be successful and fulfilled in times when many others are throwing up their hands in despair.

This STP is about courage, about fear and about failure. More to the point, this chapter is about internalizing that one single thought: "I cannot fail." As we'll see, that shift in thinking can change everything.

I think it's really important that people understand what failure means and what it is. You can either say, "I failed and I'm no good," or say "I made a mistake, therefore what did I learn? How can I use it to go on to the next step and succeed?" I don't want to sound like

102

a Pollyanna, because I know that life is not Pollyanna-ish; nevertheless, you make it what you will. If you want to use failure as a step to bigger and better things, you will. If you want to use it as an excuse for continual failure, you can do that. I choose to believe that failure means you're one step closer to success.

LARRY MANN, Aetna Life and Casualty

This Strategic Thought Process revolves around those four words: "I choose to believe." Those are words that game changers use to step outside the game of failure. They *choose* what they want to believe, and they choose not to believe in failure.

A WORLD WHERE FAILURE DOESN'T EXIST

Think of it this way. Think back on your life, when you were a teenager, or during your first few months selling. What did you *not* try because you were afraid of failing, of looking foolish, or afraid of being rejected? When you were a kid, who *didn't* you ask out, what *didn't* you try out for, because you were afraid of failing or being rejected?

Now imagine this. Imagine that you lived in a world where failure didn't exist. Where the *word* "failure" didn't exist. What would change for you? What would you be doing now if failure or, more to the point, *fear of failure* didn't exist? If both of those beliefs were not part of our mental vocabulary? If you take a few minutes to look at that issue, I think you'll agree that, as with most people, your life would be immeasurably different. Most of us would have stretched ourselves much further. We would be living our true potential, instead of living out our assumptions about our limits.

FAILURE AND SELLING

The issue of failure is critical as far as salespeople are concerned. Fear of failure and fear of rejection are the most significant barriers to success and fulfillment in selling. I've been speaking to groups of sales managers since 1960. At Wilson Learning, we've been putting on classes for sales managers for almost twenty years. Through those classes, and from listening to sales managers talk at my sessions, it's clear that fear of failure and rejection are constant companions for most people in selling. How salespeople deal with them determines to a great extent who makes it and who doesn't. Sales managers use different words for describing the barriers they see their people battling against, but the lists they make usually include the following signs of fear of failure:

Not a self-starter (so afraid of making mistakes that they don't do anything).
Afraid to ask for the order.
Afraid of calling at the executive level—high up—in client organizations.
Can't handle objections (takes objections and resistance personally).
Afraid of rejection.

BOUNDARIES TO PERFORMANCE
AND FULFILLMENT

Those *self-imposed* fears block many salespeople from performing at their best and from growing. And all those barriers boil down to the two common denominators: fear of failure and fear of rejection. These are the walls—the *imaginary* walls—that surround us.

But if we never make mistakes, if we never look foolish, if we never take a risk, we'll never grow and we'll never experience the exhilaration that exists on the other side of those fears. We become self-limiting.

THE GAME-CHANGER DIFFERENCE

Game changers typically live outside those fears. The concept of failure, of boundaries to who they are and what they can become, don't exist. They can make mistakes, they can have setbacks, they can make errors in judgment—but they cannot fail. Everything they experience helps them grow, helps them become who they are. At some level, game changers apply the words of the German philosopher Friedrich Nietzsche, "Anything that doesn't kill me makes me stronger." Failure, rejection, setbacks, mistakes cannot kill you, they can only help you learn and grow. But you have to believe that first.

They all say it in different ways and in different words, but the message is the same: Failure and fear of failure don't exist.

You should never be embarrassed or feel bad because an experiment—a sale—failed. That's not failure. You carried out an experiment and it didn't work. It is not even failure when you do a whole series of experiments, come up with a theory and then find out that there are ten exceptions to it. That's not failure. When you stop testing, stop trying things—that's when you fail, and that's when you should be embarrassed.

If I lose a sale, I lost the sale. An experiment just occurred. When I was a scientist, I did a hundred experiments to get one to work. I'm used to that kind of failure, so I'm not afraid of having an experiment—or a sale—fail. I'm only afraid of having an experiment fail by not being questioned or understood. The problem is my own understanding of why it failed.

ERIC CARLSON, Du Pont

I don't worry about failing. What can they say? They can only say no. If they do, find out why. "No" is the worst thing they can say. Actually, I like it when they say no. That's just telling me yes. I just have to find out the "why" behind the no. Then I can turn it into a yes. It's a challenge. When they come into the dealership and say, "No, we're just looking," I love it. I ask, "What are you looking for?" And the next thing you know they're buying a car.

DIANE FLIS, Buick

I think that the people who grow the fastest and probably in the most meaningful ways are the people who take failure and turn it into opportunities. My second manager at Wilson Learning had a high impact on my life. He doesn't have a negative bone in his body. Or if it's there, it's there for a fleeting second and then it's gone. If you didn't get the sale, he'd be asking right away, "What did we do wrong? What can we learn from this? How can we do it better next time?" He would always take a lost sale and ask, "What's the opportunity?" He would make it a positive experience for both the customer and us—"How can we make it Win/Win?"

DON WALKER, Wilson Learning

I've learned that it's okay to be wrong. Making mistakes is the only way you learn. Decisions are not "You Bet Your Life." If you are wrong, you're not immediately dismissed from your post and taken out and shot in the parking lot.

KATHY MONTHEI, Delta Dental Plan of California

What's the worst that can happen in selling? As one fellow said to me, "They can't bite you, they can't shoot you, they can't take your family prisoner—all they can do is not have you work for them anymore. And then you can work for yourself or someone else. Just make sure that you learn from what does not work. It would be a shame to keep making the same mistakes over and over again."

ALAN BRASLOW, Five Technologies

STRATEGIES FOR DEALING WITH FEAR

The strategy that we teach and that I use for dealing with fear of failure begins with looking inward—examining where the fear comes from. It starts with a parable. I had been thinking and writing about fear for a couple of months—I just couldn't get my arms around what I wanted to say. Then one night I had a dream; I woke up at 2 A.M. and wrote down the dream. The dream was a parable about the cause of self-imposed fear:

THE PRINCE AND HIS SERVANT

Many years ago, before the time that anyone can remember, a prince was born in the Land of Abundance. He was a favorite of the gods, so they deemed that he could have anything he wanted by asking for it in the simple and easy way they had provided.

Because he was a baby, they wanted to be sure he was protected from danger, so they gave him a servant whose name was Ego. Ego's purpose was to do everything in his very formidable power to ensure that the Prince wasn't put at risk or harmed in any way.

Ego took his job very seriously. So seriously that he decided that the best way to provide protection was to keep the Prince from making any decisions. So Ego decided to make all the decisions.

Before long, Ego the servant had become Ego the master.

And the people in the Land of Abundance were sad for the Prince. Because they knew that the gods would give him everything if he would just ask for it in the simple and easy way.

But now the protecting arms of Ego had become a prison for the Prince. Yet he was so young that he thought this was the way things were meant to be.

Then the gods looked down, and saw what was happening. And they were disappointed. So they granted the Prince a single second of insight. And he understood. And he let go of Ego the master and returned him to Ego the servant. And rediscovered the simple and easy way of getting everything he wanted.

He then discovered that what gave him the most pleasure was helping others discover the simple and easy way to get what they want. For he had discovered that everyone is born a prince or a princess.

Just like the Prince, we all have that ego that thinks its job is to protect us from all threats, real and imagined. And we also have a more rational, empowered self. The power that we all have is choice. We can choose what we want to listen to. For example, we can choose to believe the ego's message that failure is akin to the end of the world. Or, like Larry Mann, we can choose to believe that failure is simply a mistake—a *necessary* step on the winding road to growth. That choice is powerful in the implications and the potential. It sounds simple, but the ability to make those choices in tough and stressful times takes understanding and practice—it's not always easy. We first need to deal with our ego, we need to understand it, recognize it and finally let go of the power it has over us.

The Power of Beliefs

Our beliefs and assumptions determine how we see the world, how we perceive success and failure. If you're skeptical about this, try the following exercise. Below is a sentence in large type. Read the sentence once quickly. Then read it again quickly.

This time, instead of reading it, quickly count the number of *f*s in the sentence. How many *f*s did you find?

FINISHED FILES ARE THE
RESULT OF YEARS OF SCIENTIFIC
STUDY COMBINED WITH THE
EXPERIENCE OF MANY YEARS.

COUNTING THE "OFs"

There are six *f*s in the sentence. Most people see only three. The inability to see all six is very common and an example of how beliefs that *we don't even know we have* can influence what we see and how we respond. Now go back to the sentence and count the number of "ofs" in the sentence and the number of *f*s. There are six, right?

The reason you didn't count the *f*s in the "ofs" was that you made an unconscious decision—to overlook the "ofs" because they're insignificant words. You created a belief that you weren't even aware of when you read the sentence the first time. You decided what you were going to see, and that decision then limited your ability to see what was really there. *Again, believing is seeing.*

The problem is that we use the same process in selling. For example, if I choose to believe my ego's message that my clients are basically my business adversaries—out to get the best deal at my expense—I'm always going to act, think and sell from that adversarial position. *It's difficult for me to act any other way.* As long as I have that belief, I will always be coming from a position of "no trust." That's the power of beliefs.

It's time for a strategy.

LISTEN, STOP, CHALLENGE, CHOOSE

The strategy is to examine and change our beliefs. It's a strategy that is simple to understand and effective to use. That's how we can let go of our egos.

For example, think of world-class mountain climbers clinging to a vertical face, inching their way up the mountain. Most people immediately think, "There is no way I could do that! And that is exactly right. But neither could climbers if they held the same beliefs that we did. With our beliefs, climbers would also be too terrified to climb. The point is that through training, practice and repetition, climbers *change their beliefs about falling and about heights.* The mountain, the ropes and the element of risk all remain the same, but the beliefs have changed. That's exactly the process we want to go through in selling in order to disable our egos.

There are four steps involved in changing beliefs and blocking our egos from controlling. The first step is to always *listen,* to pay attention to what we are saying to ourselves. The second step is to simply *stop* when we hear our ego and its fear messages building in volume. Third, we need to *challenge* the beliefs of our ego. And finally, we need to *choose* beliefs that are in our best interests.

1. Listen to Your Self-Talk

We all talk to ourselves, every minute of every day— we call it "self-talk." But we've become so attuned to this internal conversation that we don't really pay much attention to it. *We don't think about what we think about.* Because of that, we get all these unchallenged, untrue beliefs roaming throughout our consciousness, controlling what we do and how we act. Remember, like the "ofs" illustration, beliefs that we don't even know we have influence everything we do. So step one is to listen to our self-talk, to sort out the "brainbabble" and carefully listen to what we are saying to ourselves and what we believe.

Try this:

Practice listening to yourself. Think about what you think about. Take notes. Write down parts of your mental conversation—no matter how outrageous it seems.

Especially before every sale situation, before picking up the phone to call a prospect, take a minute to listen to the conversation that's going on in your head. Don't judge, just listen in and write it down.

You'll begin to see patterns of what you say to yourself.

The second step is to analyze what you're saying to yourself. Is your self-talk realistic and optimistic? Or has your ego crept into the dialogue, saying things like "This is a big mistake" or "These people will never buy anything from me, it's not worth my time"?

Listen and then analyze. Get into the habit of listening to yourself just as you'd listen to an important client. Get to know yourself that well.

2. Stop

After you're in tune with yourself, familiar with the self-talk, the next three steps can be used anytime. For example, you're in a situation where you can feel the anxiety welling up. A presentation is not going well. The prospect's vice-president, whom you've never met, just walked into the room. What happens? You get a knot in your stomach. Your shoulders get tense. Your respiration rate goes up. The noise level in your mind shoots up.

What do you do? You *stop*. Get rid of all the internal noise, all the self-talk, and focus for a moment on yourself. Then take a deep breath. When you begin to breathe deeply, you begin to relax physically. When you are physically relaxed, it's hard to be panicky.

Watch professional or Olympic athletes. They use this simple technique all the time. It's been drilled into them by sports psychologists for the last decade. Before Navratilova serves at match point, or Magic Johnson shoots a tie-breaking freethrow or Jack Nicklaus swings on the eighteenth hole, they all take a deep breath and relax. It helps them find that calm, quiet place that takes them away from the external distractions and the internal noise.

The same skill—stopping your self-talk, breathing and relaxing—will work when that VP walks into the room. Take a deep breath and relax. Then actually say to your self, "I'm breathing deeply," and just relax. It takes only seconds. The length of a couple of deep breaths.

3. Challenge

When the internal noise and the tension have begun to subside, take the next step.

Challenge the self-talk and the beliefs of your ego. At this point, your ego is probably saying things like "This VP is going to rake you over the coals. You're not prepared to talk to him! You're going to fail!—get out!" If we listen to that voice, if we believe we are going to fail, we act that way; the defenses go up, the rationalizations spring into being and presto!—a self-fulfilling prophecy.

A CHALLENGE STRATEGY

Next time you're in a stop-challenge-choose situation, try this challenge strategy:

1. Ask yourself, What's the worst that could happen?

2. Ask yourself, What's the best that could happen? If everything worked out perfectly, what would it look like? How would you benefit?

3. Finally, ask yourself, What's realistic? What is most probable? The problem that many of us have is that when we get into a situation where we feel fearful or nervous, we don't take the time to think, to control our self-talk. When we do think it out, we usually find out that the worst that could happen is not so bad, the best that could happen is worth taking the risk, and what's realistic is worth the effort.

CHOOSING TO LOOK FOOLISH

Sometimes challenge involves admitting that it is okay to be wrong or not have the answers in front of a client. What's the worst that can happen?

My best customer in my old territory still tells this story. We were meeting, and they totally surprised me with a question. I said, "Well-ah, well-ah, well-ah . . ." about seventeen times. The best way out of it was to not be defensive and to not worry about looking foolish. After about seventeen "well-ahs" everybody knew I was in big trouble and we laughed—it broke the ice. It goes back to understanding that there's nothing wrong with saying "I don't know and I'll find out."

ERIC CARLSON, Du Pont

4. Choose

We don't have the ability to choose what's going to happen to us, what life is going to throw at us. But we do have the ability to choose what we want to believe about our circumstances. What we believe determines how we feel and how we react. In choosing the right beliefs lies all the power that we will ever need. The final element of stop-challenge-choose is about choosing beliefs.

"THANKS FOR THE TWENTY-FIVE DOLLARS."

A personal example. I brought to my first selling job a belief that was bound to get me into trouble: everybody should always love me. Obviously there are two things wrong with that belief, "everybody" and "always." And as I started selling I began to get immediate and powerful feedback relative to my belief. At the time, it amazed me to what extent people would go to avoid an insurance salesman. They would see me coming down the hall and they would turn and walk the other way. That hurt. My ego really beat me up.

My selling day would go like this: I would try to sell John, he wouldn't buy, I'd put him on my back and go see Ellen. She wouldn't buy, so I'd put her on my back and call on Mark. He wouldn't buy, and so on. By the time I got to Bill, I had all these people, courtesy of my ego, on my back. Obviously, the meeting with Bill wasn't a success. I seemed locked into that pattern.

So I made a decision. I decided to quit. No loss to the insurance industry, but admitting failure seemed pretty traumatic to me.

Fortunately, right when I needed it, a friend of mine gave me Victor Frankl's Man's Search For Meaning, *the book I mentioned in Chapter 4. That book opened my eyes to the power of beliefs. It helped me examine my own beliefs about myself and my work. A very lucky learning experience. And I made a couple of simple but powerful belief changes. I made the conscious decision to believe that no one sale would determine who I was or who I would become.*

Then I went a step further. At that time, I had to see about twenty prospects to make one life insurance sale. The average commission from that sale was $500. Five hundred dollars divided by twenty calls is $25 per call.

This is how I changed the belief game. I would call on Mary, and she wouldn't buy. Instead of putting her on my back, I'd mentally say, "Thanks for the twenty-five dollars." I would do the same thing with the next eighteen prospects. Each time they said no, I'd mentally respond, "Well, thanks for the twenty-five dollars." When I got to the twentieth prospect, and he bought, again I would say, "Thanks for the twenty-five dollars."

What happened was that fairly soon the twenty prospects became ten and the $500 commission became $1,000. At that point I could hardly wait to go out and say, "Thanks for the hundred dollars."

I didn't really change the way I was selling. I simply decided to change my beliefs. I stopped believing that when a prospect said no it was an indication of failure. And then I listened to that more rational, empowered part of myself that kept reminding me that my self-worth was never on the line in a selling situation. This became a daily ritual. I kept repeating to myself, "I cannot fail, my self-worth is not on the line."

What I was doing was controlling my self-talk, challenging the voice of my ego and choosing more appropriate beliefs. That made all the difference.

Choosing in Tough Times

It gets tough when there is a setback, you lose a sale, or your business goes under. That is when you have to reinforce your beliefs. And keep repeating it in your mind, almost like an Indian mantra, "I cannot fail, I cannot fail, I cannot fail, I can only grow and learn." When I get into situations like this, when my ego interrupts with a belief like "You blew it, and it's over," I consciously say to myself, "Thank you for sharing that, Ego," and then I go right back to choosing a more appropriate belief and repeating in my mind, "I cannot fail, I cannot fail . . . I can only learn and grow." It's in the tough situations that you have to work at choosing beliefs that are in your best interest. But that is also where the payoff is.

STRATEGY SUMMARY

1. *Listen* to your self-talk. Think about what you think about.
2. *Stop* when you feel yourself getting tense, fearful or anxious, and breathe, relax and listen to your self-talk.
3. *Challenge* the irrational thoughts and beliefs of your ego.
4. *Choose* beliefs that are in your best interests. Choose not to fail.

LETTING GO

Make no mistake about it, completely letting go of the ego as master is a dramatic shift in how we live and work. And the tougher things get, the more change we experience, the louder and the more insistent our controlling egos become. But we can let go of that.

LETTING GO OF CONTROL

I'm getting to the point where I just accept where my clients are at. I don't try to change them. You absolutely can't do that. I'm much less controlling in my calls and my meetings. I'm simply interested in finding out what they're doing, explaining what we're doing and seeing if there's a fit. It used to be that if we were even close to a fit I thought my job was to really show my clients the fit. I just got myself out of the way.

KATHY MONTHEI, Delta Dental Plan of California

That is why this is the first and the most important Strategic Thought Process—the foundation for all that is to come. The excitement and fulfillment of game changers is a direct result of their ability to let go of their controlling egos and overcome the imaginary boundaries and fears that disable other people.

"LETTING GO" EXPERIENCED

To demonstrate what we're doing to empower salespeople, help them recognize their ego, and understand the power of letting go, let me take you on a little trip, to day one of a Changing the Game in Selling program at the Pecos River Learning Center.

You've signed up through your company for a one-week sales empowerment program. There aren't a lot of details, other than the brochure saying that you should plan on doing some outdoor "unconventional" things.

Repressing your ego's grumblings about the last time you tried "unconventional" things, you show up at the Pecos River Learning Center in Santa Fe, New Mexico, the night before the session is to begin, as the sun is setting over the Sangre de Cristo Mountains. Next morning, after an early breakfast, you're ready to head for a meeting room to go to work.

But then an unconventional thing happens. A truck picks you and the other conferees up, and instead of taking you to a meeting room, it drives up into the mountains.

You come to a cliff overlooking the Pecos River, 150 feet below you. At that point you notice, with some anxiety, that there's a cable that goes from the cliff you're standing on down 500 feet to a meadow on the other side of the river. Your ego asks, at first politely, "They're not going to make me . . . ?"

Then the trainer speaks to the group. He says, "This is an exercise about limitations. More to the point, this *exercise will demonstrate to you that the limitations you think you have are self-imposed and do not exist. Everyone is going to have the opportunity, with the support of everyone, to jump off this cliff and slide down this cable, also known as the Zip Line."*

He continues, "Even though you will be perfectly safe, even though we will have you buckled into a safety harness, when you're standing on the edge of the cliff you're going to experience fear. It's the same kind of fear you may have experienced in your daily life—that may have prevented you from doing something you knew you could have done.

"For this exercise, don't try to shut it out, simply experience it and recognize it. Think of this as a model of other things in your life that you're afraid of. If you can jump off this cliff and down the Zip Line, you can do anything. That's breaking through."

At that point, he begins to explain the safety procedures and the details. But you're being visited by a familiar voice, which is saying things like "This is crazy, you could get killed! No one said you'd be doing things like this. Get your money back and get on a plane. Get out of here!" Panic begins to set in.

Then people start lining up. Although everyone is clearly scared, they all start cheering and yelling encouragement to one another. One after one, individuals stand on the edge of the cliff, are strapped into a harness and then grab onto a bar attached to a small wheel that rides on the cable. Each individual, in turn, gathers courage and then—leaps.

You, however, can't watch. Your eyes are not even working. Your full attention is caught up in an internal battle with your ego and its survival instinct. You're almost trembling with fear. The person in front of you is pale with fright. She grabs the bar, the trainer speaks to her quietly, she inches up to the edge trembling, but even as she trembles she leaps into space and is gone.

You watch her sail down the line. When she reaches the meadow, you can see her jumping up and down in excitement. She turns and waves to you to go for it!

Guess whose time has come. You're standing on a cliff, with jagged rocks and the river below you. Down at the other end of the cable, people are cheering you on.

Your self-talk is, "If you do this you're going to die." Your legs are shaking with fright, you mumble incoherently to the trainer, asking, "Are you really sure this is safe? When was the last time the equipment was checked?" (You don't want him to know that you think you're about to die.) He says to you, "Remember, this is your ego talking. Recognize it, but don't let it control you. You're perfectly safe. Find that other part of you that knows you can do it."

The cheering and the support are palpable. The noise in your head is just as loud. But then from someplace deep inside you a calm voice says, "Go for it." You leap. That leap is pure terror. But true leaps always are.

At first you fall straight down, then the cable catches and you sail across the river. The next thing you remember is exhilaration. After ten seconds you're standing at the bottom of the Zip Line. People are slapping you on the back, cheering for you. You look back over your shoulder, up to the cliff that towers above you.

That calm, connected rational part of you says, "Look at what you did. If you can do that, you can do anything."

You have just experienced the exhilaration that exists on the other side of self-imposed boundaries.

We've put thousands of people through that kind of experiential learning. We've worked with entire sales teams. The results are always similar. People simply cannot believe that they've done it. Then they make the connection that it's their ego that has been stopping them from being who they want to be and it's their ego that has been stopping them from doing what they want to do. The Zip Line acts as a metaphor. It brings all those basic fears up—everything that the ego can dish out—and people deal with it, sometimes for the first time. But they take the metaphor back to their work and use it to help them deal with all the daily fears of living or selling.

COURAGE

When you come right down to it, this discussion is another way of looking at courage. Much of what Game Changers are about is qualities like courage. The Strategic Thought Process "I cannot fail" is a way of empowering the human quality of courage—a quality that we all own as part of our birthright. All we need do is choose it. When the going gets tough, the tough let go of their egos, their boundaries and their self-imposed fear.

ACTS OF COURAGE

To bring this home at a gut level, to quell the voice (the ego) inside you that says, "This all might work for someone else, but not in my case because I have real dragons out there," let me tell you two stories. The first story, an amazing one, you may have heard, it's about Fred Smith of Federal Express. The second story, about David Stevens, whom you've probably not heard of, is even more amazing.

I want you to put yourself in the position of these individuals as you read the stories. Imagine that you experienced what they experienced. What would be going on in your mind?

FRED SMITH AND FEDERAL EXPRESS

As is already legend, Fred Smith's idea for Federal Express came from a graduate-school paper that he wrote. He got an average grade on the paper. Neverthe-less he kept his faith in the idea, he put together the company, he put his family money into it. Every step of the way he met resistance and boundaries. But he per-severed. Smith had done his research; he knew what was possible. When Federal Express started operations, they had a dismal beginning—there were times when they had more airplanes than packages. But Fred Smith kept going. He knew—he believed—that it was simply a matter of patience and perseverance for the idea to work and for the company to become profitable.

The story is told that in order to raise operating funds, he met with some bankers in Chicago to ask for a loan. The bankers, being from a profession tradition-ally short on vision and long on a need for security, turned him down. About to return to Memphis from O'Hare Airport that very discouraging afternoon, Smith noticed there was a flight going to Las Vegas. He got on it. He flew to Las Vegas, and gambled the money he had. He won enough to meet his payroll.

That's the kind of road it was for Fred Smith and Federal Express as they invented a multibillion-dollar industry. Today it's a legend and a case study that's used in MBA programs.

But right now, put yourself into Fred Smith's shoes. Hear the voices of all those bankers and other people saying "No," "It can't be done," "You're going to fail." More important, hear what his "internal" banker—his ego—must have been saying: the same fear-causing lit-any of "You're going to fail." But Fred Smith, by hook or by crook, by faith, patience and stubbornness, under-stood how to deal with all those voices, and with the accompanying feelings of fear. That's what courage is.

DAVID STEVENS AND THE MINNESOTA TWINS

This story I'm borrowing from Earnie Larsen, who is from Minneapolis and is an ex-priest and current coun-

selor doing groundbreaking work with Adult Children of Alcoholics. Again, this is a story about an individual who obviously had a strategy for dealing with fear of failure and with boundaries—in other words, he had courage:

Every year the Minnesota Twins baseball team has open tryouts just in case there's a Reggie Jackson out there who was missed by the scouting program.

A couple of years ago, David Stevens showed up for one of the tryouts. What is unusual about David is that he was born without legs.

At the tryout, somewhat taken aback, the Twins coaches asked him for a little background. It turned out that David was first in his weight class in the division in wrestling, he also played middle guard in football, and he did the sixty-yard dash in twelve seconds—on his hands. On his high-school baseball team he hit .500 his senior year.

When they asked why he came to tryouts, he said that he didn't have to be at work until two in the afternoon, so why not try out?

David Stevens lives without boundaries.

Again, put yourself in David's position. Imagine what his ego must have sounded like. Imagine the limits it would have been so easy for him to impose on himself. It doesn't take much imagination to understand that he is playing and living at an entirely different level from most of us. He has a strategy for dealing with fear. For him, failure doesn't exist.

That's courage.

Strategic Thought Process No. 1
Summary
Think: I cannot fail.

Phase III salespeople believe that they cannot fail, because for them failure doesn't exist.

Phase III salespeople have strategies for dealing with fear that allow them to keep growing and succeeding while others are disabled by fear.

Self-imposed fear and self-imposed boundaries are caused by our controlling egos.

A Strategy for Dealing with Fear:

1. *Listen* to your self-talk. Think about what you think about.
2. *Stop* when you feel yourself getting tense, fearful or anxious, and breathe, relax and listen to your self-talk.
3. *Challenge* the irrational thoughts and beliefs of your ego. Ask yourself:
   What's the worst that could happen?
   What's the best that could happen?
   What's realistic?
4. *Choose* beliefs that are in your best interests. Once you have challenged your ego, choose a belief that is rational, realistic and in your best interest.

Remember, when the going gets tough, the tough let go of their egos, their boundaries and their self-imposed fear.

CHAPTER 6

STP NO. 2: SELLING ON PURPOSE: HELPING OTHERS GET WHAT THEY WANT

THE PURPOSE OF A BUSINESS

Very important question: What's the purpose of a business? Most people's automatic answer—without their even thinking about it—is: "To make a profit." Let's take that answer a step further. When you're out with a client, do you sit down and say, "You're probably wondering about the purpose of my call. It's to make a profit for my company and a commission for myself. That's why I'm here today."

Of course no one says that. In truth, the purpose of a business is to help its clients get what they want. As a *result* of helping clients get what they want, the company makes a profit—or so one hopes. This distinction is not just a word game; it's like DNA—the order, the sequence, is crucial. Profitability—getting what you want—follows from helping others get what *they* want.

The problem is that many salespeople don't think about what they think about. They don't listen to their self-talk. As a result, although no one says, "My purpose

124

is to make a profit for my company," many salespeople *think* it. That's the thought process that is spinning around in their heads day in and day out.

PHASE III THINKING

And here is where Phase III salespeople again change the internal game. Once they've gotten their ego out of the way, they instill a specific and well-thought-out purpose. Phase III salepeople have a clear and active understanding that their purpose is helping their clients get what they want. This is not simply lip service. It's a deeply felt 100 percent commitment that is always there.

THE PURPOSE OF SELLING

I think that my purpose is to make sure that people whom I know—or will know—can provide for themselves in some secure fashion. I've had the satisfaction of delivering money for someone where the insured died too soon as well as the satisfaction of seeing someone reach his retirement age and know that without this pension plan that person would not have any money to live on. So I've done all of it now, I've designed it and I've executed it and I've seen it come to fruition. And the satisfaction is knowing that. That's what motivates me. It's not the money. It's the satisfaction of knowing that when I get up tomorrow morning there are some people that I have to see to help solve a problem that they have. And that's what motivates me.

LARRY MANN, Aetna

It's just real gratifying when you've worked really hard for a customer and they leave maybe in the first car they've ever owned, they know they got the best deal possible, they were treated well, they just feel real good about what they did and they enjoy me as a person. That's what selling is to me.

DIANE FLIS, Buick

In my work, what gets my juices flowing is to be able to provide something for my clients that they're going to look at and say I made a difference to them, I made a difference in the way they operate their company. I really believe that it's my obligation—forget whether I'm going to get paid on something or not. It's almost a lifestyle. It is really something that you either believe or you don't.

ALAN BRASLOW, Five Technologies

My purpose is to help families escape the trauma of relocating to a new city. It's such a joy to see their faces light up when you've found the right home for them. I don't sell houses, I sell a way of life. To do that, I take all the needs of my customers into consideration.

EILEEN TERTOCHA, Skipper Morrison Realty

WHAT IS THE DIFFERENCE?

Even though not one of these salespeople mentioned money, making a living is very important to them. But the connection they've all made is that the result, making a living, follows *only* if they are on purpose helping their clients get what they want. That's where they put their energies and their attention. Remember, we are talking about long-term, highly successful and fulfilled professionals. Individuals who consider helping others get what they want as their life's work—not just a way to make money.

*The main reason I'm so successful is that I put the
other person first—helping others is almost a mission.
Working any other way—working to make a lot of
money—won't work. In fact, the people who make a lot
of money aren't in it for the money. Now, maybe a few
people can get by with that, but it doesn't last for long
and if they do have the big success they want, I think
they're empty on the inside and they run out of steam
pretty fast.*

*So it's almost like a mission—to do what's best for
the other person. Almost to a fault. If another product
is just one percent better, I want the client to know
about it.*

*Personally, I could have a much smaller office staff—
just a couple of people. My profitability would probably
be better. But that's not what I'm after. I'm after reaching out, helping more people and going after bigger and
better things. I just say, forget the money, let's do this,
it's exciting. It just leaves me flat to think, Well, let's
slow down and improve our bottom line. I can't work
that way, I couldn't get up in the morning.*

*What's funny is that in the long run, working the way
I work, really mission driven, I'll be able to give away
more money than I would have made working the other
way. And, in a sense, that's one of my goals—to be able
to give away more money than anybody ever thought.*

ANN SPINAZZOLA, NorthWestern Mutual Life

THE POWER OF PURPOSE

In making this connection, in trusting it and living it,
Phase III salespeople have tapped into a source of fulfillment and performance that we call the power of purpose. Dick Leider, a life and career planner, a faculty
member of the Pecos River Learning Center and the

author of *The Power of Purpose*, defines purpose: "When I use the word 'Purpose,' I am referring to that deepest dimension of you—your innermost self—where you have a profound sense of who you are, where you came from, where you are going and how you might reach that point."

DEVELOPING THE POWER

Success and fulfillment in Phase III will be a function of working for a purpose. That purpose is helping others get what they want. To do that, we have to have three basic commitments: to doing important things, to being "of service" to our clients, and to using our own unique talents.

WHY DO YOU WORK?

I got into selling when, as a twenty-four-year-old schoolteacher with two kids, I was making $200 a month and spending $210 dollars a month. I had a $10-a-month recurring problem. I got into selling not because I was seeking my life's work, but because my uncle said I could make $400 a month in the insurance business. I thought I'd never have a financial problem again. I was lucky, because going into selling eventually took me step by step to where I wanted to go. But the sense of fulfillment didn't come until I began to make some important connections between who I was and what I did. What I began to understand was that many of us operate on two levels. There is the "who I am" level; that's the deeply personal, powerful image of who we are and what we want to be that Dick Leider was talking about. Then there is the level of "what I do"; that's our work, it's bringing home a paycheck, what we do to keep the wolves at bay. For many of us, these two levels are not connected. The "who I am" has little to do with the "what I do." Eventually, if this goes on long enough, it can cause all kinds of tension, unhappiness and frustration. More importantly, with no connection between who we are and what we do, we have no way to express our deeper selves, including the qualities of integrity, honesty and courage.

MAKING THE CONNECTION

The first step on the road to purpose is that Phase III individuals connect who they are to what they do. What they do becomes an expression of who they are. Once that connection is made, it leads to the first of three purpose commitments.

1. A Commitment to Doing Important Things

HERE TO DO IMPORTANT THINGS
Recently at Wilson Learning, we had John Allison, the President of the North Carolina Branch Banking & Trust Company, speak at our client conference. He spoke about how this sense of doing important things has transformed their bank. What he talked about was so simple and so powerful that the tape we made of his speech has become a classic in our organization and with our clients—all over the world. Here's part of what he said:
"Your mission has to be significant. If it isn't significant, it doesn't matter. Even if you literally have to change your business, your mission has to be important, because people are here to do important things. . . ."

The first commitment, then, is to getting outside of yourself, connecting to doing something important. This doesn't have to be front-page, earth-shaking news. It's a commitment to things like an idea, a cause, a client or a relationship—sometimes just getting outside of yourself.

We've all experienced this and felt how it affects our work and lives. Think back to a time when you were working for an issue that you really believed in. Maybe it was working for the development of a product or a service that you knew would be a winner—and you were ready to buck it all the way upstairs to get it produced. You knew it was important, you were working impossibly long hours, but you felt energized—turned on and awake at the end of the day. You came up against complicated problems, but you knew that the solutions were there and you found them. You were enthusiastic, happy, and you felt in charge and powerful. That's the experience of being committed to doing important things. It happens when you decide that your work needs to be connected to who you are. Because coming out of purpose, out of who you are, always leads to important things. Phase III salespeople all have a deep-seated belief about the importance of their clients and the importance of the work they do for their clients—otherwise they wouldn't do it.

2. A Commitment to Service

Game changers also believe that they serve by solving the significant problems of their clients.

Calvin Coolidge said, "Service is the rent we pay for the space we occupy on earth." That sounds idealistic, but "to be of service" is a desire that we all share at a very deep level. It is also a fundamental part of the selling purpose "helping others get what they want."

The Service Difference: Inward versus Outward Focus

If we're honest, when we look back at the early part of our careers most of us tended to spend the majority of our thinking inwardly focused. Our self-talk was: "How is this going to affect me?" "Am I going to make this sale?" "How can I make the profit margin I need?" "What if they don't like me?"

That's the Phase I and Phase II game, thinking about the "me."

What happens to Phase III salespeople is that they make the shift from the inward-focus game to an outward-focus service game. If you could hear their internal dialogue, you'd hear questions like "How can I better understand this person?" "How is this going to affect my client?" "Am I really helping them get what they want?" "Is this sale right for them? Is it priced right for them?" "What more can I do to help?" Because their self-talk is about taking care of their clients, that's what they pay attention to. Moving from "me" to "we" is part of changing the game to Phase III.

OUTWARD FOCUSED AND SERVICE ORIENTED

Before I talk to a client, I stop and ask myself, "Let's get clear, what is it you're doing?" I go through a process: I clear everything out, getting rid of negative thoughts, and I focus on the client. Are they excited? defensive? having a bad day? What is their situation today? How can I help? Then I let go of my "product pitch." I don't worry about a specific presentation. I trust that I'll know what to do.

Kathy Monthei, Delta Dental Plan of California

If you're going to sell real estate, you train yourself to listen—to hear even what the customer is not saying. That's the way that you can be of service to them before and after the sale. It takes hours of preparation, but it's worth it—customers know that you have their interest at heart. If your focus is all dollar signs, it won't work; you're not going to make it.

EILEEN TERTOCHA, Skipper Morrison Realty

From inward focus to an outward focus on service is a small shift, but it's a very profound one. It's much like seeing or not seeing the *f*s in the word game in Chapter 5. Once you become outwardly focused, service oriented, you see more options, more opportunities and different relationships than are possible if you are only focused on yourself.

Jay Messinger, of Messinger and Associates, is an aircraft broker. Working out of Houston, Texas, he deals primarily in private and corporate jets. A complex and perilous sale. What Jay does first is to focus on the client and the relationship:

In many cases, my customers initially suffer from what I call tunnel vision. That's a condition that means they have only the ability to view the salesperson as across the table, opposing them. My first job is to broaden my customers' vision and help them establish peripheral vision, thereby allowing them to see me on the same side of the table. It's a matter of perspective and focus, brought about by my purpose, which is to help my customers identify and capture opportunities.

3. Committing to Using Your Unique Talents

The final commitment needed to experience the fulfillment of selling on purpose is a commitment to using your unique talents, doing what you want do and what you're good at. About ten years ago I spent a week with a man named John Crystal, another life and career planner. John was a spy for the United States during World War II, which gives you a sense that he was cut from a different cloth than the rest of us. Since then, John has spent most of his life helping people learn his process of choosing the most appropriate career by matching who they are, what gives them the most fulfillment, to the many job opportunities that are out there. John spent the week with me working on his process. To begin, he presented the following matrix:

Hard to do, hard to learn	Hard to do, easy to learn
Easy to do, hard to learn	Easy to do, don't remember learning it

He then asked which of the four was valued most by our society. Remembering the years of "character-building" Latin classes, I said, "Hard to do, hard to learn." He agreed, then asked, "Do you know what 'easy to do, don't remember learning it' is?" No, I admitted, I didn't know.

"Talent!" he shouted. "And the problem is that most people don't value their talent because it wasn't hard to do and hard to learn. Yet," he went on, "it's what God gave them to use to make the world a better place."

That I understood—and I never forgot it.

We're always taught to work on our weaknesses. For example, for me that means work on detail! I think that's crazy. I think you go to your strengths. Realize your weaknesses, but get other people to help you with your weaknesses—let them use their natural talents in the areas where you aren't talented. That allows you to go with your strengths.

ANN SPINAZZOLA, NorthWestern Mutual Life

And that, simply, is the final element. When you use your unique talents, "Helping others get what they want" becomes the natural expression of who you are and of why you're here. Phase III salespeople are most comfortable when they are given a goal, and allowed the freedom to work and be creative in achieving it. Phase III salespeople think, Don't tell me *how* you want it done, tell me what the outcome is and trust me to get it done my way. They don't always fit the corporate mold, but they always know what they're doing and where they're going.

When I started, every deal I had was worked through a manager. I didn't do anything except what he told me to do. He would tell me what to say verbatim, word for word. And early on, it worked.

Later, I began to modify what I'd been given to say, turn it into my own words. And I was more comfortable with it, because before that I had felt like a walking robot: Everything he would say, I would say—I was a parrot.

Now I don't like being a parrot. I'm my own person. And I feel a lot stronger and more comfortable about that. For example, there are some things that, because of my personality, I just can't do. Being tough on customers, which still goes on, I just can't do—it feels as though I'm being rude and pressuring people. I can't do it. I try to run an open and honest relationship—that's my way.

DIANE FLIS, Buick

DO WHAT YOU LOVE

A simple litmus test. Ask yourself some other tough questions: Do you love what you do? Do you enjoy your work? Do you enjoy solving the problems of your clients, helping them get what they want?

Those are things that you want to love to do in order for purpose to work for you in selling, because loving what you do is a very healthy indicator of being connected to purpose.

I feel like this must have been what I was meant to do. I finally realized that this is my niche in life and it would be hard not to do it. When I see somebody so darn happy at the end, when they finally get the house they want, and they give me a big hug—that means more to me than anything else in the world. More than money in the bank.

It's my reason for getting up in the morning. It's a people business, and that's why I love it.
EILEEN TERTOCHA, SKIPPER MORRISON REALTY

Do what you love, or learn to love what you do.

To get the fulfillment and power that we've been talking about, you will have to make a choice. You can either do what you love or learn to love what you do. Loving what you do is such an intense way of living that it changes how you feel about everything, especially yourself. And the option to be doing what you love exists for everyone. It just takes some searching, some letting go and sometimes a leap of faith.

It will not work for everyone, because some people are simply in the wrong line of work. They need to change jobs. But it will work for most of us, because we are doing what we want to do, we just need a little push to get the feelings of empowerment and energy that come with working on purpose.

EMPOWERED PEOPLE MAKE A DIFFERENCE: THE NORTH CAROLINA BRANCH BANKING AND TRUST COMPANY

This is what happens to individuals when they go through a mental checklist and decide that they want to be working on purpose. As you'll see, the change can be pretty dramatic.

When we began implementing the changes at Branch Banking and Trust, the people who began the process were all three or four levels down in the organization. I was a middle manager. What happened was that one day, by random chance, we were all having lunch together. We all came to the simple conclusion that while we were all going to make a lot of money, none of us was going to be happy or fulfilled.

So we all decided to leave.

We decided to go talk to the president and tell him we were going to leave. And that's what we did. It wasn't in a threatening style, we did it appropriately: We told him that the bank was a good place for him, but it was not a good place for the rest of us and we were going to be leaving in the next month or two and we just wanted to let him know. He said, somewhat taken aback, "That's interesting. What could I change to make you interested in staying?"

We said that we really hadn't made a list, but we could come up with a few things. For example: "You have to change your whole senior management team, you have to change the relationship with the board of directors, you absolutely have to change the way you treat people, you have to change your marketing strategy and you have to have a totally different mission and view of the world."

He thought a minute, and then he said, "Well, if that's all you want, no problem." So everybody stayed, and that's when we started. It took a lot of work after that, a lot of help and a lot of change, but that's how it started.

The point is [John continued] that your CEO knows all this stuff; he knows that no matter what the bottom line is, if the people aren't self-fulfilled it isn't going to work in the long run. It's like the emperor with no clothes: Nobody has told him that he has no clothes on, and when you tell him, you find out that he knows.

JOHN ALLISON, president for BB&T

Allison and other members of the executive group of BB&T embarked on an experiment with their bank. A three-step process. First, they defined their organizationally significant purpose—in the bank's case *helping to solve their clients' financial problems.* Second, they gave everybody in the organization permission to work toward that purpose. Finally, daily, hourly, they kept revisiting, reaffirming, and reinforcing that sense of significant purpose—up and down the organizational chart and especially with the clients.

And changes began to occur. When people are working with a sense of significant purpose a lot of positive things happen, many of them unpredictable.

And so it was with BB&T's bottom line. At the beginning of the "experiment," the bank was growing at a rate of 8 percent annually in a market that was growing 10 percent. As a result of the planned changes, the executive group forecast an improvement in the growth rate to 12 percent—which would have been a 150 percent increase over the 8 percent.

I say *would have been,* because the bank's actual five-year compounded growth rate was 31.7 percent per year. That's what happens to an organization when it completely changes the game and helps its employees do what they want to do: make a significant difference by working and selling on purpose.

GETTING STARTED

If an organization the size of a bank can make those kinds of commitments, think of what an individual salesperson could do. You define your selling purpose, you revisit it daily. Keep a copy of it on your mirror, in your calendar or on your stationery. Then you allow yourself and trust yourself to work on purpose. Just as it did for BB&T, that simple sequence will change how you sell. And it will transform your results.

START LIST

1. Define and refine your selling purpose.
2. Revisit it daily, or hourly, or before every sales call. Let it change the way you think.
3. Allow yourself to work on purpose. Get your ego out of the way and keep on purpose.

PURPOSE IN TOUGH TIMES

A story to end this chapter. My father, a salesman, understood and used "helping others get what they want" during the depths of the Depression in the thirties. He was the archetypal traveling salesman. Working out of our home in Kentucky, he made calls throughout the Southeast. That meant long, dusty dirt roads, from small town to small town to small town. He sold dolls. But he did it with a difference that came from understanding what his customers really wanted and needed. He changed the game: he sold dolls as premiums.

At the time, small stores in the South were in deep, deep trouble. Hundreds were going out of business every year. My father would go into a store and talk to the owner not about dolls, but about helping the owner improve business. His idea was for the store to give away the dolls as a premium to its best customers and for large purchases. That idea caught on, and through the worst of the Depression my father was able to clear almost $1,000 a month in commissions—a lot of money in those very dark days.

All this came from understanding that his purpose was to help those store owners survive the tough times— which is what they desperately wanted.

My father told me that as a salesperson you will always work and make a living—no matter what, no matter how tough the times—as long as you keep trying to solve people's problems. Helping them get what they want. Because there will always be people who will have problems that need to be solved, and they will always need salespeople to help them. It's the glove that fits the hand. And it doesn't matter what you sell, whether it's dolls or automobiles; as long as you focus on solving other people's problems, everything else will work out.

Strategic Thought Process No. 2

Summary
Think: My purpose is helping others get what they want.

Game changers work out of a strong sense of who they are. Their work is an expression of the deepest part of themselves.

Game changers work on purpose.

Working on purpose involves the following commitments:

A commitment to doing important things, to a purpose greater than yourself. Getting outside the "me."

A commitment to being "of service" to your clients.

A commitment to using your own unique talents.

How to start:

1. Define your selling purpose. *Define,* for your business, "helping others get what they want."
2. Revisit and renew your purpose daily. Write it down, post it where you'll see it regularly. Make reading it a habit.
3. Allow yourself to work and sell on purpose—especially in tough times. When the going gets tough, let go of "I have to make this sale" and think, "How can I help this person get what he wants?"

CHAPTER 7

STP NO. 3: CREATING
WITH VISION

PHASE III SELLING IS CREATIVITY

Creativity. Vision. Those two abilities will be major components of every successful Phase III salesperson's mental toolkit. In fact, to go even further, success in Phase III will have very little to do with conventional indicators like call activity—the number of people you see. The majority of the Phase III salespeople we interviewed see far fewer prospects than most of their organization's sales force—but they are usually twice as productive. Remember the old cliché that 20 percent of any sales force does 80 percent of the business? Not only is that true, but the 20 percent does 80 percent of the business *with fewer clients*.

The difference is that Phase III salespeople understand that selling isn't a numbers game. Selling is about creativity, innovation, ideas and strategies. It's a mental game. The majority of Phase III time is spent thinking, creating and planning.

THINKING

One of the things that makes people nervous is that I spend a lot of time in my office. They ask, "Why aren't you out in front of people?" They don't understand that the majority of the work is in planning and thinking— putting all your thoughts together. I have days on my calendar for which I tell my assistant not to schedule appointments, to leave them open. I need the thinking and preparation time.

ALAN BRASLOW, Five Technologies

Don't Compete; Create!

Phase III success depends on creating the innovative leaps, the ideas that change the game on the competition, locking them out and bonding you to your clients over the long term.

Creativity is the ability to imagine and then implement the future that you want. What makes this so important now, as rapid change occurs all around us, is that creative ability, innovative ability, will separate game changers from salespeople who simply keep replicating the same old game less and less effectively.

THE BUSINESS OF CREATIVITY: PORSCHE

A Porsche slogan: "You can change the rules but you can't change the results." What makes changing the results possible is innovation and creativity. Porsche was always able to let go of the old rules and quickly learn and become the creative masters of the new game each time the rules were changed. In fact, it's because the rules kept changing that Porsche was able to stay out in front.

Peter Schutz, president of Porsche, recently brought his management team to the Pecos River Learning Center. He talked with us about how Porsche was using creativity to change their game:

What I learned from our racing experience was that if you wanted to equalize racing or, for that matter, any competitive environment, the way you ought to do it is not to change the rules for about ten years. After four or five years everyone will figure out what you're doing and then things will be pretty evenly matched.

And as a matter of fact, a company like Porsche couldn't survive in that kind of environment. We would be trampled to death by GM and Toyota and all the biggies, because they have more resources. So the way we work is by having the best people, organized so that they have permission to be creative and perform unencumbered by needless bureaucracy—if they are motivated so that they want to win; the more things change, the bigger you win. And if your plan is based on the fact that the only thing we can count on is change, you're always going to keep winning. The competition will catch on, but they won't catch up.

SEEING BEYOND THE HORIZON

Information is perishable. What we know today is useful, certainly, but it's not everything. At Cray, we have to break new ground to stay on top in our industry. What we did in the past is not good enough for the future. So we never dwell on old ideas—we're always looking for new ones. The new ideas are the future.
CHARLES W. BRECKENRIDGE, Cray Research

As Peter Drucker said, *"The best way to predict the future is to create it."* Creating it starts with envisioning it, as Peter Schutz of Porsche and Charles Breckenridge of Cray know. Fred Smith of Federal Express is another master at this. When you talk to his people, they'll tell you that Smith talks about ten years in the future as if it were the present. The possibilities of the future are so vivid to him that he sees them as a compelling and pulling reality.

Fred Smith is vision driven, a characteristic shared by entrepreneurs, and the secret of creativity.

TO THE BROWN PALACE: SEEING HOW YOU WANT IT TO COME OUT

Let me tell you about my experience about being vision driven. Without knowing really what I was doing, I had been using visualization to help me get what I wanted for most of my life. When I got into the insurance business at age twenty-three, I had a pretty good first year in selling. I became the runner-up to the rookie of the year. A lot of my success came because I had learned to use this vision power. At the time, I didn't really think of it as anything other than dreaming about being successful. I used it to daydream about making a big sale or winning a big contest. And those things then began to occur. I would get into a major sales situation and I would know what to do—*I had already rehearsed the situation in my imagination.* This ability helped me become the youngest lifetime member of the Million Dollar Round Table, selling over $15 million worth in five years. (Today that's like running the mile in ten minutes, but at the time, 1955–60, it was a noteworthy feat.)

When I think about the beginning of my speaking career, I can trace it almost directly back to the use of the vision ability. It was 1961. I had decided to try to leverage my success in selling into a career about speaking about selling. With some luck and a lot of help from Bill

Gove and Herb True, both masters of the speaker's platform, I got my first big speech for the National Association of Life Underwriters meeting in Denver.

The good news was that I got the speech, the *bad* news was that I got the speech. I had four months to worry, sweat and practice. And, in spite of a lot of effort, I had no other speeches booked before the Life Underwriters. My concern was that I was going to be "opening" in front of a crucial audience that could make or break my career.

The whole scenario called for a well-thought-out Strategic Thinking Process.

First, I had to give the event the significance it deserved. The $500 they were going to pay me wouldn't do it. There were going to be over one thousand prospects in that hall, any one of whom could book me for their next Life Underwriter meeting. I assigned an arbitrary value of $100,000 to the speech. I let that figure represent the potential booking power of the audience. That number got my attention.

Next, I knew that if I didn't do something deliberately different, I would spend the next four months worrying. It wasn't a matter of practice. It's not easy to practice a speech for a thousand people by delivering it to your mirror.

Then I remembered the *power of visualization*. At the time I only thought of it as movies that I ran in my mind. I created a sixty-second movie of myself standing before the audience at the Brown Palace in Denver. I saw myself clearly and I saw them clearly. I was great and they were great. We had a great time. I saw the ending. People were coming up, holding their business cards in their hands and asking me whether I would be so kind as to give them my available dates and fees. That was my movie. I played it every night from April to September, just sixty seconds a night.

I had never been to the Brown Palace, never even

been to Denver. But, I had planted that vision "seed" over 150 times before I got to the hall in person. Night after night. When I got there, it was exactly the same hall as in my movie. The audience looked exactly the same. I had this sense of being in perfect control, of knowing exactly how everything was going to come out. There was no fear and really no excitement. I did have a strong sense of confidence. And after the speech people came up holding their business cards in their hands, asking me whether I would be so kind as to give them my available speaking dates and fees.

That was the speech that launched my career and, subsequently, Wilson Learning.

But a lot more important to me, it was the event that proved to me that we can and do create our own futures. What I understood at that moment was that *the process of visualization* was providing the results.

THE VISION-DRIVEN PROCESS

Today, visualization and the creative process are much better understood. The critical role that the unconscious mind plays in success is better understood. Willis Harman, who wrote *Higher Creativity,* has been my mentor on understanding the process. Willis Harman: "As incredible as it seems, all we have to do is consciously program the unconscious with the correct input, and, like a mathematical formula, input plus processing time will equal output. . . . Imagery is the language of the unconscious, and the power of the unconscious is most directly invoked by the *deliberate practice of imagery and visualization skills.*"

THE LEARJET

The late Bill Lear was the developer of the LearJet. In fact, he invented the corporate jet and helped to launch modern business aviation. He also had 150 other patents to his credit. In an interview in 1975 he was asked where he got his ideas for new products. Lear replied:

First I perceive a need for a product that doesn't exist. That I take all the facts I can gather about the subject and put them into my subconscious. Then sometime later I get an answer. I believe that there is a strong outside force that sends me the answers—you can call it God, or the Superior being or whatever.*

THE FOUR STEPS

There are four steps to the creative process. First, you create the spark, asking yourself, What do you want to see happen? What is the outcome that you want? Second, you go "offline" and allow your unconscious mind to create the vision, and to create the solution. Third, once the vision is created, you use repetition and add detail, running it over and over in your imagination, like a movie in your mind, until you know the script, the actors and the locations by heart. Finally, when the vision is clearly established, when you can vividly see it out there, you take the first steps toward creating reality out of your vision.

A FOOTNOTE ON YOUR CREATIVITY
Before we go any further, it's important for you to understand that creativity is not something that you either have or don't have—no matter what your fourth-grade teacher told you. It's an ability that can be developed like any other ability. One way to start developing

---

* Quoted in *Business and Commercial Aviation,* June 1986.

*it is to remove the mental blocks that stand in the way
of creating.*

    Four common blocks to creativity are:

    *Not being aware of the fact that each of us is gifted with
creativity: it's part of our birthright.*

    *Failure to realize that all of us can do much more to make
ourselves more creative.*

    *Unwillingness to keep trying, to think up new and better
ideas.*

    *Fear of appearing foolish, or different. It's our ego that
does not believe in taking risks. But without risk-taking
there is no creativity. So in order to learn to be more
creative, stick your neck out occasionally. Sometimes
creativity lies on the other side of foolishness.*

STEP 1: CREATING THE SPARK:
WHAT DO I WANT THE RESULT TO LOOK LIKE?

The first step in the process is to ask yourself, What do
I want? What would be the best of all possible results?
Don't worry—at this stage—about whether or not something hasn't been done before, or whether or not the
technology exists, or whether you could get your manager or your company to go along. This is the internal
brainstorming session. Don't worry about all the potential problems, simply imagine the *optimum outcome.*
What would it look like? Use your imagination to explore new territories, to ask new and different questions.

What If?

Try these two words, to help you create the spark:
"What if?" What if you tried a new type of business
relationship? What if you adapted or tailored a product
that had never been adapted before? What if you tried a

new combination of products or services? What would happen? What would change? How would your client benefit? How would your company benefit? It's the scientist in us asking simple questions that result in imagining new solutions. Albert Einstein said that his talent was the ability to ask very simple—but very powerful—questions; for example, "What if . . . ?"

WHAT BUSINESS ARE WE IN?

An example of creating the spark. Porsche recently developed a new marketing strategy. It started with enthusiasm for the idea, a simple question, "What business are we really in?" and the gathering of the appropriate information.

Peter Schutz:

One of the first things I did when I began with Porsche was to analyze what the automotive revolution really was. For example, front-wheel drive, little tires, light weight, retooling—billions of dollars spent, whole new things. I looked at the cars and, sure enough, there wasn't a whole lot of similarity between what GM, Ford and Volkswagen were building compared to what they had been building. But on the other hand, I looked at Mercedes, BMW and Porsche, and nothing had changed. On a Mercedes the engine was still in the front, the transmission was still on the engine, drive in the back, four doors and a star on the hood, and it was the same way with BMW and yet they were extremely successful. So I asked myself why they weren't subject to the revolution. I came to the conclusion that I was looking at two different things.

The first group of cars, in my view, is facts-based machines. They respond to facts in the environment such as fuel cost, average size of family, average length of commute, average size of grocery package and so on.

And since many of these facts have indeed undergone a revolution, so did the automobiles that depended on the facts of their configuration.

These other vehicles, which I call nonutility vehicles, are not fact oriented, but they're feeling oriented. They depend on how people feel about themselves and their surroundings. Those had not undergone the same kind of revolution, and hence neither had the cars that depended on feeling for their configuration.

So I developed a theory that I've been talking about a lot, called "A Porsche is not a car" in which I point out that a Porsche is something that people will have even if they have nowhere to go. Our customers like to drive, and it doesn't have anything to do with going someplace. If they don't have anywhere to go, the biggest favor you can do for them is to invite them to go someplace. If you say, "Boy, I've got to go into town, would you run me in?," you know they're ready to go, because they're just looking for an excuse.

The "Aha!" that I had was that Porsche doesn't sell cars, we sell the best-engineered executive toys in the world.

STEP 2: OFFLINE

Diverge from convention. The next step is to *not think* about the situation. Let go of the belief that at this stage creativity means doing something consciously. It often doesn't work that way. We want the unconscious mind working on the problem. That happens best when we are relaxed and "offline." With the right support the unconscious mind, powered by enthusiasm, supplied with the right information, works nonstop on the problem.

TUNNEL VISION
Seymour Cray is the founder of Cray Research, the company that builds the fastest computers in the world.

Cray Research's corporate vision is simply that: to design and market the world's fastest computers. With that vision in front of them, Cray employees ask themselves daily, "Is what I'm doing right now going to help us create the fastest computers?" If the answer is no, then find something else to do that is better aligned with the vision.

Cray Research understands that the "how to" doesn't come from people working on the problem in their offices. So the designers, the engineers and the marketers have full permission to do whatever they need to do—to go offline—in order to be creative.

For example, rumor has it that Cray himself had wanted a tunnel under his house ever since he was a kid. So he is digging a tunnel under his yard. He spends a lot of time digging his tunnel and that is where he gets his ideas, where he does his "offline" learning. When he sits down at his desk, he writes down the ideas that he had while he was digging his tunnel.

With the vision of creating the fastest computers, Cray trusts that he will come up with ideas and answers. Digging his tunnel helps him take his mind off line so that the unconscious mind can create.

When I wrote my first sales training program, Sales Sonics, in the early sixties, I kept misunderstanding how the creative process works. I would go to my office, close the door, sit down and try to come up with ideas. It didn't work. Lots of coffee, time and paper were consumed—but no ideas were created. Finally I would get frustrated and I would walk away, because nothing was happening. But then I made a simple discovery. I would lie down on a couch, go "offline," relax, listen to Judy Garland records (I know that dates me) and not think or worry about it—and the ideas would pour out. That's how creativity works.

So take time to muddle around and to go off in tan-

gents. Creativity doesn't work on a schedule and it doesn't always come to work. Get out of your office, don't sit around staring at a yellow legal pad. Find your own way to free your unconscious mind.

The creative act owes little to logic or reason. In their accounts of the circumstance under which big ideas occur to them, mathematicians have often mentioned that the inspiration had no relation to the work they happened to be doing. Sometimes it came while they were traveling, shaving or thinking about other matters. The creative process cannot be summoned at will, or even cajoled by sacrificial offering. Indeed, it seems to occur most readily when the mind is relaxed and the imagination roaming free.*

FROM THE BOOK *AHA!*, by Martin Gardner

Trust

Going offline and developing your unconscious ability means trusting yourself. *Trust that you are creative, trust that the vision or the idea will come.* Believe that you are creative, and don't panic. The idea, the vision, might not show up on schedule, but it will show up.

More people get block here because they stop believing that it will happen, they stop believing that they are creative. Their ego intrudes, telling them to stop this foolishness and go back to work. The most important thing you can do is shut off that voice and trust yourself.

You'll be lying in bed in the morning, barely awake, and pop!—it will be there. The perfect outcome—the connection that you've been searching for.

This is going to sound really crazy. But when I'm on my way to appointments, a lot of times, just the opening

* Quoted by Morris Kline in *Scientific American*, March 1955.

sentence that I'm going to say comes to me. It's weird. More times than not, things will kind of just come to me. All I do is try to relax, review a file and think about a few things. It's uncanny—it just sort of comes to me.
ANN SPINAZZOLA, NorthWestern Mutual Life

STEP 3: RUN THE MOVIE IN YOUR MIND

The next step is to create a detailed and vivid "movie in your mind" of the outcome. What does it look like? If you're visualizing a meeting, what does the room look like? What do the participants look like? What are they saying, what are they thinking? The key is detail, specific. What does it sound like? Feel like? Smell like? Get all your senses involved.

MOVIES
A few weeks ago, I closed a big sale with Bob Hope. At the closing, I had a picture of him and me taken in front of his new airplane that I had just delivered. After I had it developed and started showing the picture off, someone asked me when did I take the picture. I told him, "About four months ago," He said, "Wait a minute, I thought you just closed the airplane the other day." I proceeded to tell him that I took that picture in my mind four months ago when I began working with Bob Hope. Closing on the airplane was just having the picture developed.
If I had not had that picture in my mind, I wouldn't have followed the steps in between to make the sale.
JAY MESSINGER, Messinger and Associates

I see the end result—that somehow this person is going to leave here, they're going to drive out in a car.

*I just keep thinking and thinking and thinking that. I
see my prospects writing a check, sitting in the business
office doing the financing—the whole thing.*

DIANE FLIS, Buick

*I've learned that I can create a purpose, populate it
with visions and take myself to something new through
the sheer force of creativity.*

*For example, I had a situation where another com-
pany had handled this large school district account for
years. The school system didn't want to change carriers,
but I said to myself, "Is what I'm offering good for
them?" The answer was yes, so I came to the conclusion
that they ought to have Delta Dental Plan of California.*

*I created the specific vision of them buying our plan.
I thought, "We are going to do this . . . this is a given . . .
I'm here to fulfill their destiny." I constantly banished
negative thoughts from my mind and concentrated on
the outcome I wanted. One and a half years later, they
bought Delta Dental Plan.*

KATHY MONTHEI, Delta Dental Plan of California

Specificity and Repetition:

Be as specific as you can. Visualize all the details of
how the optimum outcome will work, look and feel.

Use repetition. Keep playing it over and over in your
mind. Get into a regular habit. Before you go to sleep,
or just after you wake up in the morning, play your
movie. Regularly, religiously, repeatedly.

For example, the Australian twelve-meter sailing
crew that beat the Americans in the 1983 Challenge Cup
used visualization as part of their preparation for the
race. Each crew member visualized the races, their specific roles and their victories. Each did that every night,

fifteen minutes a night—*for two years*. That's repetition, and the payoff was, of course, that they were the first team ever to beat the Americans.

Repetition is one of the keys to unlocking the power of the human mind. Just as repetition in exercise strengthens muscles, so the repetition of a mental movie increases the power and pull of vision.

The Vision Process

Step 1: Create the Spark. Ask yourself, what do you really want to have happen? What is the optimum outcome? Get all the information you need, take the time to think about it, then write down the options you develop.

Step 2: Go Offline. Stop thinking about it. Relax. Trust that the vision will come. Let your unconscious mind process the information and what you want to have happen.

Step 3: Run the Movie in Your Mind. Paint a picture as vividly and as detailed as you can of the outcome you've envisioned. Be as specific as you can. Visualize all the details of how the optimum outcome will work, look and feel.

Use repetition: keep playing it over and over in your mind.

STEP 4: FROM VISION TO REALITY

Once we have that specific and compelling movie in our minds, moving it to reality requires commitment and an understanding of the importance of first steps.

Commitment and Focus

The Spanish explorer Coronado, upon reaching the New World, burned his boats, committing himself and his followers to the exploration—there was no way back. That kind of commitment, made up of trust in your vision, your personal power, and a lot of positive self-talk is the first requirement for moving your vision to reality. You need to be 100 percent committed to your vision in order to move it through all the setbacks and all the frustrations (the organizational immune system) that always accompany the word "new."

A MODERN-DAY BURN-THE-BOAT STRATEGY

Seymour Cray, of Cray Research, builds a boat every year. He sails the boat for the summer, and at the end of the season he burns it and begins building anew. Sounds awfully labor intensive, but here's the strategy: Having the old boat around cannot help but influence the building of the new boat—for better or for worse. What Cray wants to do is commit to building a new boat. He thus burns the known in order to commit himself to his new vision.

GETTING FROM HERE TO THERE

Ray Bradbury, the science fiction writer, said, *"First you jump off the cliff and you build your wings on the way down."* Once you've committed 100 percent to the vision, it's time to trust 100 percent that you will build your wings and fly before you hit the ground.

What's your first step? You've got this compelling vision; how do you move it to reality? Let's say that you've got this great idea for a specific application of a product; what's next?

With that vision clearly in front of you, move in the most appropriate direction. Move even when you don't have all the answers. Don't expect to be right the first time. The operating principle is "Ready, shoot, aim."

THE DEBUGGING PRINCIPLE

When I speak about creativity and learning, I usually ask how many people in the group have ever programmed a computer. A few hands usually go up, and then I say, "Those of you who have programmed computers know something that the rest of us don't." I ask them, "After you've written your program, and you've turned on the machine, what happens?" The universal answer is that it doesn't work. What do programmers do? Do they get upset, do they quit or trash the entire program? Of course not. *They've learned not to expect any program to work the first time.* Instead, they "debug."

With the outcome you want clear in your imagination, you take that first step. Once you've taken the first step, you "debug": you make corrections, you alter your course based on learning from the first step.

Remember, a plan is simply a starting point; you can never really be sure how you're going to get to where you're going. The best you can hope for is knowing where you are going. At the Pecos River Learning Center we bet our clients that they can't show us a plan that ever worked as drawn up. Plans are always altered, modified and rearranged by reality. In getting from vision to reality, we need to accept the same reality, that there is no such thing as a straight line. Just like navigation, getting there is a process of fits and starts, of finding yourself off course and correcting.

158 / Changing the Game

LEARN-HOW VERSUS KNOW-HOW

"In a time of drastic change," wrote Eric Hoffer, "it is the learners who will inherit the future. The *learned* find themselves equipped to only live in a world that no longer exists."

What this chapter is really about is another Phase III quality: creativity. We also call it "learn-how." In rapidly changing times, that's the survival ability: always taking the stance of the learner. Always being ready, able and willing to discard the old game for the new. In fact, being out on the edge inventing the new game. Out ahead of our competition, sometimes out ahead of our own organizations.

As our clients demand more and more innovation, we cannot be satisfied just to respond, just to be reactive. We need to be able to leap ahead. To be creative and innovative. Always be willing to use "What if" to replace "This is the way things are." Game changing means gut-level understanding that knowledge is the enemy of learning and that learning is the key to creativity.

"Know-how" was the old game. "Learn-how" is the new.

Strategic Thought Process No. 3

Summary
Think: Creatively create the vision.

Selling in Phase III is about creativity, innovation, ideas and strategies. It's a mental game instead of an activity game.

The ability to be creative and innovative as rapid change occurs all around us, as the game and the rules keep changing, will be what separates game changers from salespeople who simply keep replicating the old game.

THE CREATIVE PROCESS:

1. Create the spark. Ask yourself, what do you really want to have happen? What is the optimum outcome? Get all the information you need, take the time to think about it, then write down the options you develop.
2. Go offline. Stop thinking about it. Relax. Trust that the vision will come. Let your unconscious mind process the information and what you want to have happen.
3. Run the movie in your mind. Make a mental movie of the outcome you've envisioned. Be as specific as you can. Visualize all the details of how the optimum outcome will work, look and feel. Use repetition: Keep playing it over and over in your mind. Run it in your mind regularly, every morning or every night.
4. From vision to reality. Keeping the vision of the outcome in front of you, move in the direction that seems appropriate. Debug, make changes, learn from every mistake.

CHAPTER 8

STP NO. 4: LEADING
THE TEAM

How does a salesperson with no position power create, direct and manage a team sale? Not just the formal team, but the informal teams. How do you get the product support people, the accounting people and the shipping department to work—with 100 percent support—on your team, work on your vision? How can you make that happen when no one reports to you?

When you don't have position power, you need to have influence, empathy, personal power. In a word, leadership.

FROM THE LONE RANGER TO LEADERSHIP

As business becomes more complex, with more buyers, more team sales and longer sales cycles, success in selling will be tied to leadership ability. For salespeople, with or without position power, leadership means qualities like trust, vision, commitment, courage and accountability.

This Strategic Thought Process is about those qualities and that kind of leadership. About making the thinking shift from the Lone Ranger "me" team, out there doing it all alone, to the leader of the "we" team.

LONE RANGERS TO LEADERS

Business today is very competitive—we've all got competitors out here who sell the same product, that can do the same thing. If I'm out there representing just myself, if I'm the only interface that the client has, then the only thing it takes to knock me out is a salesperson who is better than I am. Or a problem that I haven't been able to solve but they can. But if I have developed the line relationships from their person who places orders to our person who takes orders, and to their scheduling people to my scheduling people to every part of their organization, then my competitor has to knock my organization—and that's a different game.

ERIC CARLSON, Du Pont

I'm a sports buff, so I think of myself as the quarterback, managing the people and the process for my clients. When I started with this account, I was the lone salesperson. Now there are seven salespeople working on the account, plus an enormous array of support people at our home office. In order to truly manage an account at this level, I learned a long time ago that I don't have to know everything—what I know is not important. It's knowing what other people know, especially the resource support personnel who represent specific areas of expertise, and who bring that expertise to the client. The point is: you can't do it all yourself.

DON WALKER, Wilson Learning

"I HAVE TO DO IT MYSELF—BUT I CAN'T DO IT ALONE"

This shift, from Lone Rangers to team leaders, was brought home to me recently when we put on the annual sales meeting for a medium-sized company. We had just completed what we call the "ropes-course" day—a full day of outdoor learning activities. We put around a hundred salespeople through rock climbing, the Zip Line and other similar activities. It was the end of the day; the sales force was sitting around a fire, barbecuing, drinking beer and talking about what the day had meant. After about an hour, an individual stood up and said that he had spent part of the day casually observing a couple of the high performers, just to see what was different about them, as they went through the course. This was his "Aha!" He watched the high performers—especially two of the women, who were in the top five in the company—consistently and constantly ask for help, advice and support. He went on to say that until that day he had believed that top performers in selling were soloists—and that was the role that he had tried to play. But a day of watching his "role models" ask for and receive support changed his vision of high performance. He understood that not being able to do it alone was an admission of strength. That getting support and giving support to others was the new role of the high-performing salesperson. That understanding is the start of the shift from "me" thinking to team thinking—part of Phase III.

When I was with this other company—earlier in my career—it was, internally, an adversarial situation. The salespeople and the conversion people were at opposite ends of the building—literally—and it was war. "Sales sold it and conversion made sure it didn't work"—that was the theory.

Today it's a lot different. Every sale is the result of teamwork. From the telemarketer who has me talk only to prospects who are qualified—who want to do something—to the technical-support person who makes sure that we can deliver anything we promise, to the "hotline" team that makes sure that we deliver the after-

the-sale support I promise, to the product-development
group that keeps us ahead of the pack—that's my team.
Without them I don't think I'd have the strength that I
have in the selling cycle.

Teamwork is the key to our credibility and success.
We all succeed because we truly care about delivering
what the most important team member, the client, be-
lieves they are purchasing.

Too many salespeople go it alone and never realize
true success in selling. That won't happen to me or my
clients.

ALAN BRASLOW, Five Technologies

Leadership Ability

This is an entirely different role from what most of us
learned "growing up" in selling. But it's clearly one of
the key abilities to success in the future, and it doesn't
matter what you sell. If you're a sales manager in a car
dealership, you're dealing with service people, administrative people and the finance manager. You want 100
percent effort from those people—not simply just doing
their jobs—and especially you don't want them working
against you.

What will make the difference is that some salespeople will be able to inspire, motivate and establish
bonds with the people they work with, while other
salespeople will send memos, make requests and then
try demands. The latter group will get frustrated when
nothing happens.

The difference will be leadership.

PHASE III LEADERSHIP

The first step in exploring leadership is exploding an
important myth about what leadership is and what it

isn't. Next we'll look at the characteristics of leadership, how true leaders think and work. Real leaders are skilled in many of the STPs we've already discussed. They know how to get their ego out of the way, how to work on purpose, how to create a vision and how to inspire people with their vision. Finally, they are masters at giving 100 percent support to a team and allowing the team to support them.

To start, it's important to understand what leadership is.

The Leadership Myth

There is a myth about why people become leaders and what motivates them. When I speak to groups of managers or facilitate manager workshops, I have them do a leadership exercise. I ask them to tell me why they think people want to be leaders. I've done this exercise over and over again, and invariably I get the same responses. Most people say, power and control. The other things I hear a lot are words like "money," "status," "recognition." I group these into a category called "wanting to be served."

Then I ask them to go back in their personal experience and remember when they were in the presence of a leader who affected their life. That one special teacher, coach or first manager. I ask them to describe the motives of those leaders.

What they remember about those leaders is that they seemed motivated to give power, to free up individuals to see more options and potential. Finally, the leaders they remembered were motivated by wanting to serve instead of to be served.

At the end of the exercise, groups are faced with a 180-degree difference between their perceptions of why people become leaders and the motives of the leaders who made an impact on their lives.

LEADERSHIP: MYTH AND REALITY

The myth is that effective leaders desire power, control and to be served. The reality is that leadership is motivated by a desire to be of service and to give power to people.

If that reminds you of the purpose of selling, you are exactly right. Selling and leadership are connected— different applications of the same intent, serving and empowering people.

Leadership Intent

The first step in understanding leadership—or selling —is understanding your intentions, understanding why you want to lead or manage. Is it to have power, or to give power? Is it to be served, or to serve? Is it an ego-driven game? Or is it driven by a deeper sense of purpose, of wanting to help others get what they want?

Leadership, in its most powerful and compelling form, will not work without positive intentions. A positive intent, a focus on others instead of on self, is the foundation of leadership. Without that foundation, all the skills, techniques and trappings of leadership will ring hollow; people will always sense the contradictions, and they will never give 100 percent support—they will always have a backdoor.

But when the positive intent is there, all the skills and the characteristics of leadership will naturally follow. Just as in selling, intention and purpose make up the foundation on which everything else is built.

THE FOUNDATION OF THE TEAM

Our team is made up of the right people in the right jobs. My husband's and my job is helping them reach their full potential and realize that they are equals in our business. Just because I can sell doesn't mean that I should get all the recognition and such. It's like quarterbacks in professional football. The good ones know that if they didn't have the players in the line, they wouldn't be anywhere—they'd be dead. And that is exactly where I'd be if I didn't have our team.

ANN SPINAZZOLA, NorthWestern Mutual Life

THE CHARACTERISTICS OF LEADERSHIP

Effective leaders seem to share four main characteristics. First, they understand and use the power of vision. Second, they know how to share and communicate the vision. Third, they see their task as facilitating, running interference for and empowering the members of the team so that each member of the team can work on his or her part of the vision. Fourth and very important, leaders lead by example and constancy. They inspire people with their integrity, accountability, patience and courage.

Characteristic No. 1: The Leader as Visionary

Warren Bennis, author of the book *Leaders* and our leadership expert for the Pecos River Learning Center, interviewed ninety leaders from all segments of the public and private sector. One of the characteristics shared by almost all of the ninety was their ability to create compelling visions. Visions that excite other people, that they wanted to play a part in. They can see a new product, a new relationship or a new company so clearly that other people get hooked. Warren says that leaders capture attention through vision—they get everyone excited, they make it fun.

LEADING THROUGH VISION AT PORSCHE

This comes from Peter Schutz, the president of Porsche. Peter was instrumental in helping turn Porsche around in the early eighties. Besides being an astute business person, Peter is also a leader—understanding and using the power of the vision to lead.

I started my job with Porsche in January 1981. That first February I saw my first sports car race at Sebring in Florida. There was this car there called the Porsche 935, which was a roaring turbo-charged monster. I'd never seen one—and fifteen of them completely dominated the race. It was only a question of which one of them was going to end up winning. I got back to Germany—I tend to get very emotional—and I was just like a teenager, I was so excited.

I got all the people from the racing department together and told them about what I had experienced, and they sort of looked at me and they knew they were in trouble. Because if I could get that excited about that kind of race, well, it was clear to them that I didn't understand anything.

I asked them to tell me what was the most important race of the year. They said the twenty-four-hour endurance race in Le Mans. And I said, "Wonderful. How are we going to do there?" They told me that they were preparing a car called the 924 GT and about some of the problems they were having with the gaskets and so on.

Finally, I asked them what were our chances of winning. "Well," they said, "Mr. Schutz, you don't seem to understand. The 924 GT is not powerful enough to compete with the prototypes and the other race cars and, besides, that's not the point of the race. The point of the race is to prove the durability and reliability of the Porsche car."

This—of course—was the opening. I said, "Well, folks, as long as I'm president of this company we will never go to a race without the objective of winning— that's our vision. Now this meeting is adjourned, and I want you back in my office tomorrow at ten and with a plan on how to win that race." And that was only two months—sixty-two days—before the race.

A most remarkable thing happened. First of all, our director of research and engineering pulled me aside— he had been with the company for thirty-three years and really was the heart of the technology—and said, "You know, Mr. Schutz, I hope you understand that the work you have just authorized is not in our budget." And I said, "If we win that race, no one will ever ask us the cost. If we lose, then we'll have a problem and we'll have to deal with it."

Anyway, the next day they came back and they had all the answers. They said, "We have some cars, called 936s. They're in the Porsche Museum. They once won the race. Of course, they're no longer competitive. But," they continued, "we developed an engine that was sup- posed to race at Indianapolis. That program was also canceled, but we saved all the pieces." They went on that they would have to convert it from alcohol to gas- oline and that they could use a transmission from a Porsche 917.

Then they said, "If we do that, we might just have something."

The next thing that happened was that a few days later the phone rang, and a man at the other end said, "Mr. Schutz, you don't know me, but my name is Jackie Ickx. I'm retired, but I've won Le Mans four times, and if the rumors I hear are true, then I would like to drive my old car." Within the next forty-eight hours, the top *endurance drivers in the world had called up and said they were ready to drive. And, incidentally, not one of them talked about money. The point is, when you have exciting projects you get the best people.*

We created a vision and they followed us—and we went on to win that race.

But it goes on from there. After that year—1981— they changed all the rules. And the result was that we had to design a completely new car, the type 956, which we finished a few weeks before Le Mans in 1982.

We went to that Le Mans with three 956s. They were numbered one, two and three—and that is exactly how they finished after twenty-four hours. In fact, they did the last lap in echelon—a bit of nonsense, but they were demonstrating their dominance.

After the race, the press got me aside and said, "Tell us, Mr. Schutz, how do you explain this? Three brand-new, untested cars and you totally dominate the race. How do you explain this?"

I said, "You're missing the point. You see, the cars are new, but the people aren't. They are the same crew that won last year."

Characteristic No. 2: Communicating the Vision

Leaders understand how to communicate each part of the vision to their team. Everyone clearly understands the roles and his or her importance to the team. From the administrative assistants all the way up the ladder, everyone understands the big picture and their roles in it.

This is *not* the salesperson who blows into the home office waving the biggest contract in corporate history, with directives and demands for shipping and order entry; those people get compliance—if they're lucky. True leaders see individuals, not roles; they work with people, not titles. They go out of their way to establish personal relationships, not simply reporting relationships.

SHARING THE VISION

I often ask our people to look at the bigger picture. I've nurtured my internal clients, like order entry, administrative support and product development—I consider them as important as my external clients. Sharing the vision is part of the nurturing. You have to share the vision with the people you work with. It's very important that their purpose, their mission, is very close to yours when they are working with the client.

Your goal is to build teamwork that serves the client in the most effective manner.

DON WALKER, Wilson Learning

ASKING, LISTENING AND RESPECT

Very specifically, some of the common verbatim comments that Warren Bennis heard about leaders was that they listened and asked questions. When they communicated, they *communicated*—they didn't simply "tell." They asked for everyone's opinions and comments. Further, they respected opinions and were always willing to acknowledge and use. better ideas than their own. Within the broad parameters of the vision, they let go, they didn't control. They let other people play as big a role as possible.

CONTROLLING, LISTENING AND LEADERSHIP

Two related stories about this aspect of leadership. They come from John Pound, of Montgomery and Andrews, a Santa Fe attorney and friend. Both stories are about working with teams. The second story is about true leadership.

Cutting Out the Local Guy

The first story is about how not to do it. John's law firm was investigating its first large word-processing system. A very large national computer firm had one of the systems being considered. John and the other people on the buying committee had worked with and liked the local sales representative. He was a native New Mexican and he understood how things work in New Mexico, which is somewhat different from the other forty-nine states.

But this potential sale was big enough for the computer company to send a team of people from the regional office to make the presentation. When the team arrived, it was clear from the onset that they had not talked to the local guy and had not included him in on the strategizing. It was clear that the computer company's team leader was control oriented, he was going to leave nothing to chance, he was going to run everything his way—the company way.

Even though it was scheduled to be a relaxed evening meeting, the computer team showed up in their three-piece suits. The clients, however, were all sitting around in jeans and cowboy boots. As John relates, the impression was that they were just one more presentation to these guys and that it was just dollar signs that counted.

As the computer company's sales manager made his presentation, they never allowed the local person to present. He just sat there in the background. The problem was that the local guy happened to be a friend of most of the members of the client team and they noticed that he was being discounted.

Although the facts, the prices and the competitive analysis information were heard and were major reasons that the law firm went with a different vendor, the lack of caring, supporting and simply listening took *their toll. It came down to "Don't tell me how much you know until I know how much you care." The attorneys didn't like the way the sales manager cared for the local guy.*

Ted Kennedy: Listening and Leadership

Soon after that presentation, John had the opportunity to work with Senator Edward M. Kennedy as he campaigned for the 1980 Democratic Party nomination for President. Kennedy was scheduled for a tour of New Mexico. Now, you might think that in New Mexico someone as well known as Kennedy might make a couple of speeches about national issues and then depart. But not Kennedy. He showed up and gathered all the Democratic leaders together for one day, locked in a room, and asked questions about local issues, local politics, local traditions and taboos—and he listened. Names, places, issues: he took all in.

When he went out to make his presentations, in a state that is almost as far removed from Washington, D.C., as possible (local wisdom says that the only thing New Mexico has in common with the rest of the country is the currency), Kennedy spoke about local issues, he talked about the local candidates, whom everyone knew. He was sensitive to the local politics and the local differences.

He understood that the leader's first task is to listen, to understand, to ask questions, then to give support.

New Mexico has never been an important political state as far as national elections go. That made Kennedy's commitment, his willingness to learn and understand—his leadership abilities—even more apparent. He didn't win the national nomination, but he did win the New Mexico primary.

Those two stories contrast what leadership is and what it isn't. Leadership is not telling, ignoring or or-

dering around the local people. It's listening, sharing, asking questions and empowering.
That's the leadership difference.
Try this approach at the next meeting you lead. Once the agenda is set, the purpose of the meeting understood, do nothing but ask questions and listen. Try facilitating and clarifying instead of running the meeting.

See each participant as an individual who wants to contribute, not just as the person from Order Entry. Listen and understand all the ideas, even the ones that you disagree with. Respect people's time, end the meeting on schedule. Listen and learn the local politics, the local dos and don'ts. Empower the team.

Characteristic No. 3: Empowerment

Leaders give people power; they help people see their own potential—no matter what the growth might mean to the leader or to the project. In fact, leadership could be boiled down to that one operating principle: helping people grow, helping them remove the obstacles to growth no matter where that growth might lead them.

Art Grayson, of Grayson Pontiac in Knoxville, Tennessee, is an example of this kind of leader. I first met Art at the Pecos River Learning Center, where he and his entire management team participated in one of our Team Building workshops. Art will tell you that the success of his business is very important to him, but his biggest kick is in watching and helping people grow, giving them permission to make mistakes and learn from them. For example, Art had an assistant sales manager with a lot of potential, but the young man just didn't seem to be comfortable in his job. He was so afraid of failing that he wasn't doing anything. Without telling him what to do, Art told him to go out and do what he thought was right, to make mistakes (leaders rarely use the word "failure"). Art said, "If you do something wrong, we'll tell you, but go out and do what you think needs to be done." Art took all the self-restraints off this assistant sales manager, and it turned him around—he is now on his way to being a high performer. Give support and people will grow.

Characteristic No. 4: Walking the Talk: Courage, Perseverance, Patience, Accountability

Another characteristic that impressed Bennis, and that was shared by the majority of the ninety leaders he interviewed, was they *were* their principles. They didn't talk about courage and patience and accountability, they lived it. One of the individuals Bennis interviewed was Admiral Hyman Rickover, the father of our nuclear-submarine fleet. Rickover told Bennis that he had lived through 250 separate hearings and eight years before the first nuclear sub, the *Nautilus,* was approved and constructed.

Bennis called that courageous patience—having that clear vision, communicating to your people, and then personally having the patience and the courage to see it through setbacks, random events, discouragement and disappointment.

What makes these qualities so refreshing is that today —in the midst of change, complexity and ambiguity— they are so rare. Leaders who live and lead by these values stand out. They inspire trust and they motivate performance.

Review: The Leadership Characteristics

1. Leaders create a vision of what could be, to inspire and motivate people.

2. They know how to share and communicate the large picture of the vision and each individual component of the vision.
3. They facilitate, run interference for and empower the members of the team so that each member of the team can work on his or her part of the vision. They help people grow.
4. They lead by example. They inspire trust with their courage, integrity, accountability and patience.

THE ART GRAYSON STORY

The new leadership model is the "we"-driven leader instead of the "me"-driven leader. And that's where Art Grayson rejoins us. His story, of moving from manager to leader, from "me" to "we," is a classic, step-by-step example of what leaders do.

A few years ago, Art wrote up a list of all his responsibilities as the owner and manager of the dealership. He then went around to his managers and compared notes. What he found was that most of the items on his list, the day-to-day management of the dealership, were being taken care of by his department managers. As Art said, that's when he understood that his role had changed. He decided that he needed to make the transition from manager to leader in order to build a powerful team at his dealership. So he began reading about and exploring leadership. And then he took action.

Step 1: Create the Vision of What Could Be

First Grayson and his managers got together and jointly developed a vision of what they wanted to become. They came up with three components. First, they wanted to be a strong developer of people—they wanted to hire and train people who could grow in the business. Second, they wanted to lead their market in customer satisfaction. Finally, they wanted to change the tradi-

*tionally highly adversarial customer–salesperson rela-
tionship to one of trust.*

Step 2: Communicate the Vision
*Art then decided that he needed a powerful team-build-
ing experience for his managers. He brought them to
the Pecos River Learning Center for four days of team
building. As Art relates, they accomplished more team
building in that intensive four days than he had been
able to do in five years. At the end of the four days, his
managers were committed to supporting each other, to
trusting each other, to bringing fun back to the dealership and to reducing the "Rolaids level" that existed in
that very tough and stressful business.*

Step 3: Empower Your People
*By now, Grayson's people began to assume their power
—with his 100 percent support and help. They had a
meeting on what to do next. It was scheduled to last an
hour. It went on for half a day. They decided that the
next step was to get the rest of the employees involved.
They took a risk and shut the dealership down for a half
a day and then took everyone to dinner—to celebrate,
to inform and to ask for participation. To the people in
the trenches, events like this signify that change is real,
that the leaders are serious. The message was that they
wanted everyone to be involved. In order for the dealership to succeed, they needed everyone to grow, to develop and to be a part of the team.*

Step 4: Walk Your Talk
*Grayson is a model for the vision, the support and the
trust. Right down to the specific, the day-to-day "how
we do business." A small example that illustrates the
power of walking your talk: A customer bought a 1979
Mustang with a one-year warranty. The warranty was
supplied by a separate warranty company. After ten*

thousand miles the engine went bad. The warranty company said that the engine was just worn out, no parts were broken, and they refused to back the warranty. Grayson and his service manager huddled and decided to take over the responsibility and overhaul the engine. Integrity, customer service and value added—just what we've been talking about. But the story doesn't end there. Grayson had a new, cynical service writer in the dealership. He had come from a tough, adversarial union-shop factory. The new service writer had no intention of buying into the new vision or culture. In a small dealership, one person with that kind of attitude can do a lot of damage. But seeing that the owner of the company meant what he said, even when it meant spending money, turned him around. The new service writer "got it," because Grayson and his managers walked their talk; they acted with honesty, integrity and courage. Art told me later that getting that service writer turned around paid for the cost of that engine overhaul.

Art Grayson came up with a vision, empowered and supported his people around the vision, and then got out of the way. His intention was to help his people grow. That's leadership.

LEADERSHIP IN SELLING

The same characteristics apply when your task is to lead a team of people through a sale. You create the vision of what you want, you share the vision with your team, you empower your people, and you assist each one of them in working with accountability on his or her part of the vision. Finally, you persevere, you lead with integrity, courage and patience.

It takes discipline, especially for salespeople who cut their teeth on going out there and bringing it back alone.

It takes a shift in thinking, from "me" to "we." As business gets more complex, with more people involved in larger deals and longer time frames, we cannot do it alone—it isn't possible. We need to make the shift in our thinking from Lone Ranger—"I'm out there doing it by myself"—to team leader, getting supported by giving support. That's leadership. That's a Phase III selling quality.

Strategic Thought Process No. 4

Summary
Think: Leader of the team, not "Lone Ranger."

The Leadership Myth:

Leaders desire power, control and to be served. *The reality is that leadership is based on a desire to be of service and to empower people.*

The Leadership Characteristics:

1. Leaders create a vision of what could be, to inspire and motivate others.
2. They know how to share and communicate the large picture of the vision and each individual component of the vision.
3. They facilitate, run interference for and empower the members of the team so that each member of the team can work on his or her part of the vision. They help people grow.

4. They lead by example. They inspire trust with their courage, integrity, accountability and patience.

The essence of leadership is moving from "me" to "we."

CHAPTER 9

STP NO. 5: PARTNERING

If you were to ask Phase III salespeople to describe the client relationship that they see in their minds and aim for as a goal, you'd hear words like "mutually beneficial" "empathic," "long-term," "strategic," "interdependent." The word that we use is "partnering." Phase III salespeople are masters of the partnership.

THE PARTNERSHIP DIFFERENCE

The best way to get a sense of what "partnering" means is to look at how the buyer–seller relationship changes as salespeople grow in their careers.

Phase I salespeople tend to think that their clients are adversaries—to them it appears that their *clients* stand between them and success. "Get the money and run," "Get them to sign the contract," "It's them versus us" are the kinds of internal slogans that are running around, often unchallenged, in the Phase I salesperson's mind.

The Phase II salesperson moves out of that adversarial game. He or she is a problem solver. But a very focused problem solver. As a Phase II salesperson, I have to make sure that my clients' problems match up with my solutions. Their square peg has to fit into my square hole or we have nothing to talk about. The Phase II job is really to go out and find clients with the right-shaped peg. Because of that tight focus, Phase II salespeople tend to miss the larger strategic opportunities. Further, when the relationship gets rocky, when negotiations get rough, many Phase II salespeople go right back to Phase I survival, the adversarial mentality.

Then we get to Phase III salespeople. They've completely changed all the rules of the selling relationship. In the first part of this book, I said that if we ignored titles and companies, stepped back and looked at what was going on in a Phase III relationship, it would be hard to tell for whom the Phase III salespersons work, their company or their client.

And that's the difference. Phase III salespeople are so close to their clients, so good at understanding and anticipating their needs, so responsive to their clients, that you think they are on their clients' payroll.

"REMEMBER WHO PAYS THEIR SALARY"
Stan Schmitt, development programs manager at Du Pont, has a wonderful story about how even individuals who work for Du Pont can misunderstand the economics of selling:

I know of at least three instances where a business manager or vice-president has gone out to make calls with some of our top salespeople. Most of these people consider themselves to be "customer oriented." And yet, on the plane heading back to Wilmington, they'll turn to the salesperson's boss and say, "You know, you're really going to have to watch out for that salesperson, because he's getting a little too close to the customer. He's got to remember who pays his salary."

Of course, the punch line that Stan usually delivers is, "By the way, who does pay his salary?"

THE STRATEGIC ADVANTAGE

What's the advantage of being that close, of being partners instead of just out solving problems and moving on? The simple principle is that vendors cannot compete against partners. The vendor, selling the one-shot solution, cannot compete against the salesperson who has developed and nurtured a long-term, mutually beneficial relationship.

Of course it takes strategic patience and a different kind of attention and commitment to form a partnership. A salesperson has to move the relationship inch by inch in that direction. But what Phase III salespeople understand is that it is such a competitively strong strategic position that it's always worth the effort. A partnership locks out the competition.

Repeat and Referral Business

Another advantage, as I mentioned earlier, as selling gets tougher and more competitive, success for organizations and salespeople will depend on repeat and referral business. *No one will succeed in selling without repeat and referral business.* That means satisfied clients coming back and it means satisfied clients referring their friends and acquaintances. The only way that will happen, especially with sophisticated consumers, is if they believe that your intent is positive and they know that you are there for the long term.

It doesn't matter whether you sell at the corporate level or to individual consumers. The insurance salesperson says, "I'm not here to sell you a policy, but I'm here to be your lifelong financial adviser." That's a financial partner. The automobile salesperson says, "I'm not here to use you to move my quota, I'm here to be your transportation consultant for as long as you are buying cars." That's a transportation partner. Beliefs like that change the game in those professions—and that is what success in the future of selling will require.

It's clear that what makes this work is purpose and integrity. When clients experience it, they want to share the experience with their friends, relatives or associates. But it works only when you're committed to this approach. Remember, today more than ever we live in a small world. Nothing travels faster in our small world than bad news—or a bad reputation. Not working with integrity, or not being 100 percent client oriented can ruin you faster than anything else. The most important credential we have—outweighing competence, product knowledge and the lot—is our reputation for integrity, honesty and client service. That makes everything possible—including the opportunity to obtain repeat and referral business.

I work so closely, in such a close little nest even though Dallas is a large city, that if I were not to pay one claim everyone in my market would know about it. I guarantee they would. Because that one person knows fifty others who know fifty others. So I have to be very careful. I have to be sure that I volunteer all the information to them and make sure that they volunteer all the information to me. This is why I can't work for people I don't trust. No one sale is worth my career. But

if I trust them and they trust me, then there's a mutual
relationship that we can keep coming back to.
ANN SPINAZZOLA, NorthWestern Mutual Life

THINK: EMBER

The essence of partnering can be summed up in one
phrase: *establishing mutually beneficial, empathic re-*
lationships. It doesn't matter what you sell, the key to
partnering begins with EMBER. When you think of em-
bers, you think of a warm, long-lasting glow, as opposed to
the quick flash in the pan which is a more appropriate
metaphor for much of traditional selling. Thinking
EMBER begins with asking questions like, How can I
make this a long-term "glowing" relationship? How can we
both benefit? Thinking empathically, What do my clients
want from this relationship?

LONG TERM

It begins with a salesperson seeing beyond the quick
sale and the fast opportunity. Letting go of short-term
thinking to see the range of other possibilities. The
problem is that in many industries short-term thinking
is so strong and pervasive that very few salespeople get
the opportunity to experiment with anything else.
For example, in the consumer industries salespeople
are hit over the head constantly with the myth that selling cars or small computers is a one-shot, short-term sale
—that there is no such thing as a "Be Back." Short-term
thinking in our profession—just the pressure to close
deals quickly, to hit our numbers—can influence us in
very negative ways. Sometimes it's the relationship that

suffers, sometimes it's quality, and very often what suffers is our ability to see other—larger—opportunities.

A while ago, I taught a sales managers' workshop for a company in the recreational-camping industry. During the seminar, it seemed that every thirty minutes a sales manager would get up, go to the phone, call the office and ask how many deals had been closed in the last few hours. It occurred to me that I was watching twenty sales managers addicted to the short-term, quick-hit belief. A belief reinforced by their company. Like all addictions, hard to break, and very harmful to future success. It takes a courageous, intuitive and bright salesperson to break through that belief system and see other possibilities.

Try this. Take a prospect whom you're currently working with. It doesn't matter whether you work with cars or computers. Instead of asking yourself, How can I close this business by the end of the day, month or quarter?, ask yourself, What could this relationship look like in three years? Or five years?

What would you do differently if a three- or five-year relationship was your goal? How would your customer benefit? How would you benefit? What would change? Would there be less pressure to make a fast sale if you were looking for repeat business? Would less pressure help the way you worked? Would it help create a better relationship?

Changing your thinking from short term to long term can fundamentally change the way you work.

Obviously, "long term" means different things in different industries. But no matter what the industry, the opportunity to change the game—the length and the productivity of the relationship—exists. The result of that kind of change can redefine the potential that exists in your business.

Believe me, I know how this sounds, especially if

you're sitting there with big numbers for this quarter staring you in the face. I've been there. I've worked this problem from every angle—as a salesperson on quota in good times and in bad, and as a CEO of an organization that was driven by making quarterly numbers. But I also know that success over the long term will depend on our ability to break through the boundaries of short-term thinking and concentrate on developing strategic, long-term partnerships.

THE STRATEGIC, LONG-TERM ATTITUDE

Phase III salespeople do so much more long-term thinking. They have thought out—not just thought of— what to do in situations that are months away. And they have everyone, whether it's the customer or Cray management, already pre-positioned for what's going to happen. The critical situations, either internally or externally, aren't difficult to deal with. They've all been thought out months in advance. That's strategic thinking.

MIKE WILHELM, Cray Research Western Region
general manager

To sum up, mastering the long term starts with your own thinking, with letting go of the short term, stopping and analyzing what it is about the short-term game that motivates you. Next, challenge what it is about the short term that gets in the way of really stretching yourself to think long term. Once you've got all that out on the table, the final step is to choose. And the Phase III choice will predominantly be the long-term game.

SELLING AUTOMOBILES AND THINKING LONG TERM

A dramatic example of long-term thinking—a game change—comes from the industry that traditionally has been one of the most "flash in the pan" short-term oriented: the automobile industry.

As you read this, remember that Diane Flis sells on
the average of 300–350 Buicks a year—250 percent over
the industry average. And much of that comes from her
ability to establish relationships with her customers
that last two or three years into the future. Understand
how Diane works and you'll understand how she has
changed the game in selling cars from a short-term,
walk-in business to a long-term strategy.

Having someone drive away in a new car is the end
result. But it starts by thinking, How am I going to get
there? Where will my business be coming from? It
might not walk in that front door, so I have to generate
it on my own.

I have a game plan when I come in every morning. I
write down the names of the people I'm going to contact, by letter or by phone, the people I'm going to follow up on, and the people I'm going to thank for
sending me business.

I handwrite letters to follow up on existing clients;
that's two or three hundred cards a year times seven
years—it's a lot of people. It takes me forever, but I don't
forget those people's names or the kinds of cars they
bought, and they don't forget me. I keep referring to my
client files two, three, four times a year when I do my
mailing. I can remember people from seven years ago
who came back in only because I took the time to send
them a card every year.

Now, this is the repeat and referral business that all
the other guys who sell cars are never going to see.
They're missing the boat. They have to chance it with a
marginal "up" coming in the door. Some of these people
have twenty years in the business and I still sell more
cars than they do.

The reason is that 80 percent of my business is either repeat business or referral business.

I've had people whom I worked with five years ago, who didn't buy a car from me, come back because I've helped them remember me for five years. They came back and bought a car after five years.

Diane Flis works on establishing a long term trusting relationship with her prospects and customers. That's something different from most automobile salespeople, who are out in the lot with the sole objective of trying to move cars *today*. Diane thinks EMBER and it pays off.

MUTUALLY BENEFICIAL EMPATHIC RELATIONSHIP

"Mutually beneficial" and "empathic" go back to purpose, helping others get what they want. It means always coming from the empathic point of view, walking in their shoes, asking yourself, What does this look like from my client's point of view? What do they want? What will they want in three years, in five years? This means leaving all the vestiges of adversarial thinking behind forever, sometimes acting and thinking as if you are on their payroll (which, of course, you are), even when the going gets tough—*especially* when the going gets tough.

THE RELATIONSHIP MANAGER

Thinking EMBER is a step up in complexity and sophistication from the one-on-one, one-shot vendor sale. In a partnership, the salesperson plays the role of leader not only for the salesperson's company, but also for the individuals in the client's organization. The salesperson leads the teams and orchestrates everyone through the complexities of contractual, legal and financial issues that need to be addressed.

But the most important role that salespeople can play involves managing the relationship, creating the relationship around which everything else occurs. That means never losing sight of the big picture and working constantly on keeping the trust level high.

THE KEYS TO A PARTNERING RELATIONSHIP

There are three keys to a strong partnering relationship. These are the keys that relationship managers pay attention to above all else. The three are shared values, alignment on purpose and vision, and 100 percent support.

1. Shared Values

One of the most effective means to bring about a partnership is to get right to core corporate beliefs—to discuss, share and get agreement on the values of both organizations.

If your client discovers—with your help—that both organizations share *and practice* some basic values like quality, respect for individuals or others, it goes a long way toward creating a solid framework from which a powerful partnership can be built.

When I call on our clients, whether they are new relationships or existing accounts, that's the level of conversation I like to get to as quickly as possible.

For example, around 1968, Wilson Learning brought the idea of "win-win" to the marketplace. We felt that both the salesperson and the customer should benefit from working together. That's what we believed and that's what we taught. At the same time, we were working with the distribution division of a major automobile manufacturer. We were in the process of developing a fairly large sales training program with them. But when we got down to a discussion of values it became clear that we had a problem. Their people, who worked with the dealerships, believed in "moving iron." They mandated what the dealerships would sell, how many and by when. They were not really interested in hearing the perspective of the dealerships. Clearly not a win-win relationship.

As far as we were concerned and they were concerned, this was a fundamental conflict in values that would keep coming up and make the development of a sales training program impossible. We respected each other's points of view but agreed to disagree, and both companies walked away from the table.

Fifteen years later the same division came back to us because, over those fifteen years of radical change in the auto industry, their values had changed. "Win-win" was now an important part of the relationship they wanted with their dealerships. And because of that they remembered Wilson Learning. The point is, sharing values, creating a match at that level, automatically deals with a lot of the traditional items that interfere with business relationships. When clients sense that we share the same value structure, questions about our propriety, our intent, our dedication and our competence tend to fade away or get flushed out so that we can deal with them directly.

In a long-term partnership, basic values need to match.

TASTE: THE SHARED VALUES OF A PARTNERSHIP

In the team-building workshops that we do at the Pecos River Learning Center, we've come up with five basic values, "TASTE," that are critical to partnerships as they are to teams. In our work, we have the teams openly discuss and get agreement on the following:

100 percent Trust: Everyone understands and trusts everyone else's intentions. Everyone commits to a mutually beneficial relationship and to trusting the others.

100 percent Accountability: Everyone takes 100 percent personal responsibility for the partnership, for the success and the setbacks.

100 percent Support: Everyone commits to giving and receiving support. Our slogan is 100 percent support through all the mistakes until we get it.

100 percent Truth: No holding back of information or opinion. A willingness to talk about anything. This is especially true for bad news—the delays, the price increases and the rumors.

100 percent Effort: Everyone is 100 percent committed to the mission. You don't go into meetings with one eye on the door. Or with the intent of making sure the meeting ends at three, so that you can catch the only direct flight home.

These are ideals, targets to shoot for, to constantly be revisiting and using as a touchstone when the going gets rough. It takes practice and role models and small steps, but once you've established a 100 percent relationship it's virtually impossible for anyone else to compete against it.

At the Pecos River Learning Center, we give teams permission and protection to "try out" operating under these values for a week, to get a feeling for how dramatic the change can be.

2. Alignment on Purpose and Vision

Everyone involved in the partnership—all the team members from both organizations—needs to clearly understand the purpose of the partnership and be committed to the vision. Everyone has to agree on where they are going.

Further, the individual partnership members must believe that they are coming together to serve a purpose higher than just a contract between a vendor and a client. They need to believe that the partnership will make a difference to their organizations over the long run. The task of the leader/salesperson is to create—or to assist the team in creating—this clear and compelling vision.

In a number of partnering situations where I was involved, we've taken the time up front to get everyone together, all the buying influencers, everyone who was involved. We've gone around the table and had everyone describe the optimum outcome that they could imagine. What would it look like in three or five years? When and how would they know that their expectations were being met?

It always amazes me what comes out of this kind of session. Not only do you get all kinds of ideas and creativity, but you also get a very powerful group of people committed to a common vision.

3. From Selling to Supporting

In a long-term partnership the role of the salesperson moves from selling to supporting. The salesperson in a partnership is actively and equally concerned with the growth, health and satisfaction of everyone involved.

THE PHILOSOPHY OF SUPPORT

A partnership is a marriage. It's the highest level of a relationship with a client that I believe a salesperson can achieve. In a sense, it's a very intimate relationship, because it has to be established on trust. Trust—on both sides—has to permeate the relationship. . . . The difference between partnering and selling is that partnering is not loving and leaving, it's loving and staying. It's similar to a family relationship. Their pain is your pain. When they feel it, you feel it.

There is an intense camaraderie, support and understanding that borders on love, because you can go through tough times together. It's deep caring and respect.

All of these people whom I deal with have their careers on the line, and so do I. They have little or no opportunity for advancement in the organization if our projects are not successful. As a salesperson in a partnership like this, you share pain as well as success. If they fail, you fail. You stay in the partnership with them—you support them, their failure is your failure, their success is your success.

DON WALKER, Wilson Learning

What you do in the supporting role can be all over the map. But the *thinking* is the same. It starts with keeping our egos out of the way, making sure our focus is outward, on the welfare of the partnership and the individuals, rather than on ourselves. Always asking of everyone involved, "What can I do to help? What do you need? Are your expectations being met?" That's support.

THE KEYS TO A PARTNERING RELATIONSHIP

1. Shared values.
2. Alignment on purpose and vision.
3. One hundred percent support.

THE PILLSBURY-KRAFT PARTNERSHIP

One of the most interesting, long term, mutually beneficial partnerships that I'm aware of exists between

Minneapolis-based Pillsbury and Kraft, Inc. Tony Sherber, Pillsbury's vice president and general sales manager of their U.S. Foods division, his people, including a few salespeople from Kraft, were recent visitors to the Pecos River Learning Center and they shared the story of the partnership with us.

The partnership began in the thirties in Louisville, Kentucky. At that time, the biscuit company that Pillsbury eventually acquired, had just begun to make and market a prepared-dough package of biscuits. The problem was that the biscuits had a relatively short shelf life without refrigeration—they literally blew up after a few days unrefrigerated. Since transportation to all the small stores in the region took a fair amount of time back then, this was a serious problem. The company, not having the resources to invest in its own fleet of trucks, looked around to find out who was already using refrigerated trucks—what existing distribution system was available. The answer was a company then known as the Kraft Cheese Company. Kraft was distributing cheese in refrigerated trucks all over the region. A partnership was struck—one that grew to national proportions and one that Pillsbury inherited and strengthened after they acquired the prepared-biscuit company.

But dramatic increases in cost of material, and increased profit competition, began to take their toll on the business in the seventies. Market volume began to erode, profit margins began to slide. The stage was set for changes in the way the business was managed.

Enter a Phase III salesperson—a relationship manager.

Ray Kimery brought decades of experience in the Pillsbury organization when he moved into the refrigerated-food group. But he also brought something else to the table. Ray was one of those individuals who in spired great loyalty in the people who worked for him. As Tony Sherber, who once worked for Ray, relates, he would chew you out in the morning and then take you out for a beer after work. Ray was a leader. You always knew where Ray stood and respected his opinions— even if you disagreed with him. Ray was prematurely grey and throughout the Pillsbury organization he was known as the "Grey Eagle."

In 1980, Ray was given the task of revitalizing the Kraft-Pillsbury business. After analysing the situation, Ray came to the conclusion that both companies needed to first reinvest, in terms of money and attention, in the basic business. That was the strategy that he decided to sell to both partners. His first "sale" was to Pillsbury. He convinced the Pillsbury board to take a time out— to take no growth in profits from the Kraft relationship for two years. That money would be reinvested in the business. His next sale—just as difficult—was to Kraft. He asked Kraft to change the entire relationship with Pillsbury. Since the thirties Kraft had been a distributor of Pillsbury products. Kraft bought the products from Pillsbury, added its margins and resold them to the retail outlets.

Ray had to convince Kraft that the only way Pillsbury could stay in the business was if Pillsbury controlled the pricing and invoicing. He asked Kraft to change from being a distributor of Pillsbury products to being a broker, where Pillsbury did the pricing and paid Kraft a commission—a major change and for Kraft, a major risk. But Ray was convinced that both companies would make more money and see the business grow in the long run if his strategy was adopted.

Acting more as an ambassador between the two organizations, he asked both to "let go" of the way business had always been done in order to help the partnership grow. The money and attention re-invested

*went into new technologies, new products and Ray Kim-
ery's "gold standard"—a new quality definition for re-
frigerated-dough products.*

*Ray Kimery's task was to manage this delicate rela-
tionship, to make sure that everyone's needs were met
through the transition.*

*The risk, and new partnership paid off. Under Ray's
stewardship, and others who understood his vision,
after eleven years of decline in the business, the Pills-
bury-Kraft partnership enjoyed five consecutive years
of real growth.*

*The relationship first, meeting everyone's needs, long
term thinking and 100 percent integrity. That's how
Ray Kimery thought and worked. A Phase III salesperson creating a Phase III partnership.*

Strategic Thought Process No. 5

Summary
Think: Partner instead of vendor.

The key to partnering is thinking Establishing Mutually
Beneficial Empathic Relationships—EMBER.

Key Points:

1. Think long term. Ask yourself, What could this relationship look like in three years or five years?
2. Become a strategic specialist. Become fluent in your
   client's strategic objectives, decision process, growth objectives and politics and culture.

The Keys to a Powerful Partnership:

1. Shared values. In a long-term partnership, basic values
   need to match.

2. Alignment on purpose and vision: Everyone involved in the partnership—all the team members from both organizations—needs to clearly understand the purpose of the partnership and be committed to the vision.
3. One hundred percent support. In a long-term partnership the role of the salesperson moves from selling to supporting. The salesperson in a partnership is actively and equally concerned with the growth, the health and the satisfaction of everyone involved.

CHAPTER 10

STP NO. 6: VALUE ADDED

Value added is about exceeding expectations—going beyond the job description, getting outside of the box. Let me start this chapter with a story that I always remember when I think about value added.

THE MACARTHUR STRATEGY

I was in Japan, working with Caterpillar-Mitsubishi, one of our large international accounts. I was having dinner with one of their executives, and I casually asked where he was from. He said Hiroshima. As you can imagine, my first reaction was "gulp." But we were fairly close, and so I asked him if he would mind talking about it.

He said it would be fine with him, and then he went on to tell me that when the bomb was dropped he was away but his family was at home. It was thirty days before any word came out of Hiroshima about survivors. He naturally assumed, and it was confirmed by the authorities, that his entire family had been killed.

As it turned out, the authorities were wrong. Their

198

house, for whatever reason, was still standing. His family had survived the explosion. After the bombing—out of wisdom, or by incredibly good fortune—the family left Hiroshima and avoided death by radiation. Another family moved to the house, and they all were killed by radiation sickness. A very powerful experience. But he went on with the story, and this is the part that always reminds me of exceeding expectations.

My Japanese friend told me that when the war was finally over, the Japanese received a complete and total surprise. I asked him what he meant. He said that after the surrender the Japanese knew that the Americans were going to treat them horribly—it was what they expected because that's what the Japanese had done when they had been the occupying force.

What then happened, he said, was incredible. The Americans came in and began cleaning up, treating the wounded and feeding the population—exactly the kind of thing you would do for your best friends. He said they were amazed. "I want you to know," he said, "that our relationship with the United States began right there—incredible trust was created at that moment. We rebuilt, we became friends, and we became bonded together as countries—all out of the war."

That entire strategy, he went on, was Douglas Mac-Arthur's. It did not come out of Washington. MacArthur completely changed the victor–vanquished relationship, by exceeding the expectations of the Japanese, and thus created a powerful ally.

NOTHING NEW

In selling, adding value isn't a new concept. In fact, it's been a centerpiece of Wilson Learning's sales curriculum since 1965. Most successful salespeople practice value added. The difference is that most salespeople use value added occasionally, sometimes by luck or happenstance. Game changers have made the unusual usual. They practice value added constantly. Mentally asking the question "How can I add value?" is part of their standard operating procedure.

GIVING THIRTEEN FOR TWELVE

From the day I started in this business I've always felt that if I do what's right for the client, eventually I'll get paid. People say, 'How can you do all this?' I say, 'Because it's the right thing to do. I'll get paid somehow. I don't know how, but I'll get paid. And just look at me—it's worked.'

I think that what I do is I give people thirteen when they asked for twelve. I think that's the reason I've been as successful as I have been.

LARRY MANN, Aetna

That is the philosophy of value added. To put it in the words of another game changer, valued added is *always* working outside of your job description in order to exceed the expectations of clients.

THE COMPETITIVE EDGE

Operating beyond your job description, always exceeding the expectations of your client, is the perfect way to change the game on your competition. When you go beyond the expectations of clients, leaving your competition believing that the game is about measuring up to expectations, you've effectively locked them out of the new game.

They won't be locked out forever, because people are pretty smart and they will always figure out what you're doing. But that isn't important. What is important is understanding the strategic process of adding value. If you understand and use the process, you will always be changing the game ahead of your competition. They'll catch on, but they'll never catch up.

Value added is the Phase III competitive strategy.

KNOWING IT WHEN YOU SEE IT

Value added is somewhat like the Supreme Court's opinion on pornography: Pornography is hard to define, but you know it when you see it. Because of that, we've come up with value-added stories from all sorts of industries to illustrate the rich variety of actions that are value added. They range from small actions to large ones. But the thinking is always "How can I exceed my client's expectations?"

VALUE ADDED IN SELLING REAL ESTATE

In general, we try to make moving as easy as possible, so that the transition from city to city works smoothly. I tell them, "I'll take care of all the details for you, you can go to your new job with a perfectly free mind." I'm very detail oriented—there are so many things I can do for my customers, like arranging financing, connecting utilities, ordering homeowners' insurance, securing a decorator, or referring professionals like doctors and dentists.

I give my customers first-class treatment on moving day, including plenty to eat for both the family and the movers. Then, on a regular day-to-day basis, I check to see if everything is going okay or if they need any help from me or anyone else.

All this just makes them feel that somebody cares for them. And that's important, so they know that they are

not alone in their new city and that they have a friend
they can call day or night.

      EILEEN TERTOCHA, Skipper Morrison Realtors

More about Eileen, from one of her clients:

As a sales manager, I can appreciate professionals.
Eileen is indeed a professional and a pleasure to work
with. We've moved six times in eleven years but have
never enjoyed a new-home purchase more than this one.
The best part of all was Eileen's follow-up in taking
care of all the little details, making this the easiest move
we've ever made. She went beyond the call of duty when
we discovered some roof leaks on a Saturday night and
she appeared on our doorstop with our insurance agent
and the builder in tow in order to solve the problem.
That extra effort, well after the purchase, really im-
pressed me. Now I use that incident to help train all our
new salespeople.

WHAT VALUE ADDED ISN'T

Because the customer's expectations are always increasing, today's value added is tomorrow's expectation.
For example, things like prompt delivery, responsive
follow-up, and personal calls are not value added. That's
just good (not great) service! If you're involved in simply
meeting customer expectations, like 80 percent of the
salespeople and companies around today, the only way
to be profitable and to be competitive is to be the least
expensive. That's the game of submitting bids and hop-
ing that you have the lowest price, of constantly worrying that your bid will be beaten by a cheaper but equal
product. A very hard, grinding game.

As John Allison from North Carolina Branch Banking and

Trust pointed out, if you can't be the low-cost producer
—and, in reality, most of us aren't—you have to be a
value-added producer.

THE THREE STEPS TO CREATING
VALUE ADDED

The Strategic Thought Process question asked before
every meeting or sales situation is "How can I add value
to this sale?"

Being able to come up with the answer quickly and
effectively requires some homework first. There are
three steps to being able to think "value added." The
first step is creative. It's re-discovering what business
you're really in. The second step is breaking down that
"big picture" into small value-added opportunities. The
final step is to put all those opportunities through an
evaluation process in order to select the most appropriate and cost-effective ones.

If this sounds a lot like the creative process, you're
right. Value added and creativity go hand in hand.

CREATIVITY AND VALUE ADDED

*Value added is creative thinking while serving the
client's needs. If I can't think creatively, it's difficult to
offer value-added services, because then I'm looking at
the client and the interaction with blinders on. That's
like saying "There's only one way to do it, sorry. Our
company rules and regulations won't allow it."*

*Value added is often getting outside of company rules
and regulations. It's getting outside of the nickel and
dime decisions. It's thinking long-term, big decisions
and big opportunities—it's risk-taking. The important
thing is that we exceed the expectations of the client.
You never want the client to ask, "Where's the versatil-*

ity? Where's the value added? Where's the creative thinking of this organization?"

Creative, value-added service will separate you from your competition. But most importantly it will serve the client's needs, often beyond original expectations.

Don Walker, Wilson Learning

Step 1: What Business Are You in?

Remember the old saw that if the railroad companies had understood they were in the transportation business, not the railroad business, they would still be in business today? Being able to make that jump—to understand what business you're really in—is the first step to understanding your full range of value-added offerings.

Understanding your business begins, paradoxically, by forgetting your product. You're not the computers you sell, or the cars you sell, or the financial services you sell. As Marcelo Gumucio, the executive vice-president for marketing at Cray Research says, you sell dreams and you sell solutions; you simply deliver product.

Put on your marketing hat and ask yourself, What do my clients really buy? What do they really need? When you understand that, you'll understand what business you're really in.

AN ANSWER TO A DREAM

Our clients have dreams. They dream about simulating the behavior of atomic nucleii and studying the earth's atmosphere. They dream of designing a car that is completely safe. They dream of modeling airflow over an entire aircraft, of studying alternative oil-recovery operations, of predicting weather days in advance. So the appeal of Cray machines is tremendous. Because they know that the payback is huge. Imagine being able to extract 10 percent more oil by using a Cray system— that could mean billions of dollars to a petroleum industry customer! Our customers are all dreamers, and it's at that level that we really work.

Marcelo Gumucio, executive vice-president for
marketing, Cray Research

Every product or service can be looked at that way. For example, one of my big breakthroughs in the insurance business came when I realized that I wasn't selling insurance. I became much more successful when I understood that I was really selling a deep sense of satisfaction that comes when individuals know that they've taken care of the ones they love. Once I understood that, I began creating and targeting value-added actions toward that end instead of just selling insurance.

Step 2: From the Big Picture to Value-Added Actions

Once you understand the business you're really in, the next step is to ask yourself, "What actions can I take that will add value to my offering—that will exceed my clients' expectations? What can I do that will position me as different from and more valuable than my competition?

Creativity again. Take whatever time you need—offline, with a lot of trust in yourself, no interruptions— and put the questions to yourself. The answers you get may not be earthshaking, they may be very simple—just actions that no one else in your industry is considering.

VALUE ADDED IN SELLING AUTOMOBILES

I handwrite all of my correspondence: thank-you letters after people pick up cars, thank-you letters if they come in and don't buy, and thanks for coming in and

*giving me the opportunity to help purchase a car. The
envelopes are handwritten, I don't type a thing, nothing
is computerized.*

*I started sending thank-you letters if they didn't buy,
just because I enjoyed meeting the people. I really enjoyed working with them, and a lot of them left with
the attitude that if they didn't buy a car here it was
really nice talking with me anyway.*

*The thing is, I hate junk mail—so I won't send it out
to my prospects and clients. Instead, people see something handwritten, they say, "Wow!"*

DIANE FLIS, Buick

Step 3: Value-Added Evaluation

The final step in the value-added process is putting
your ideas to the reality test. Ask yourself questions like:
How can I bring this idea to my clients? Can I afford to
do these things? How much will it cost? Does it duplicate any other service we provide?

When you put all your ideas through this kind of evaluation, maybe only a few will survive, but those ideas
will be on purpose, reality based, and they will help you
exceed your clients' expectations. And that word will get
around—that's the payoff of value added.

*VALUE ADDED IN HUMAN-RESOURCE
SOLUTIONS AND SOFTWARE*
*Before I worked for Five Technologies, I specialized
in payroll systems for large companies. I had a client in
the cosmetics industry who was going online with us.
The controller's biggest fear wasn't that we couldn't do
the job, but that our company was going to be sold or
something of that magnitude would happen (the random event) that would affect the decision he made and
he would look foolish and lose his job. I told him, "If*

that happens, if I find out that our company is going down the tubes, I'll be the one to pull the string and find you an alternative solution so that you won't have a problem."

ALAN BRASLOW, Five Technologies

A word of caution. As you evaluate your ideas, ask yourself the question, Is this value-added action going to mean more work? The answer sometimes will be yes. But don't reject the idea based on the amount of work. Instead, think about the payoff. Think of how it will position you in the marketplace and how that position will save you an enormous amount of time, energy and money over the long term. The point is that value added, like partnering, leadership and leveraging—which we will look at in the next chapter—are Strategic Thought Processes for working smarter, not necessarily harder. But it takes some effort up front to get the ball rolling.

VALUE ADDED IN SUPERCOMPUTERS

We don't want to merely meet customer expectations, we want to exceed those expectations. In addition to first-class systems and service, then, we must deliver a lot of intangibles as well.

Let me give you an example. We collect performance data on our systems daily, and one time we noticed some problems with one of our computers at a customer site—a $10 million machine. We told the customer that this machine wasn't meeting our standards, even though the customer was satisfied with its operation. So our executive vice-president (EVP) of operations went out to visit the client and assess the situation. The customer said that although some minor problems existed, we could leave the machine in place—they could live with the problems. Our EVP replied that we couldn't do that—we would take the system back because we were *dissatisfied with it, and we'd ship them a new system free of charge. The customer was stunned.*

But we also do little things. Most of our systems are shipped from our Chippewa Falls, Wisconsin, manufacturing facility with some of Chippewa's famous Leinenkugel beer. You know, we send the beer and they can have a party. Receiving this system is a major event for the customer. It's a major event for our on-site personnel too. And the beer party at system-installation time helps build an incredible relationship between the customer and our people.

MARCELO GUMUCIO, Cray Research

VALUE ADDED REVIEW

Step 1: What Business Are You in? Rediscover what business you're really in and what your clients really buy. See the "big picture."

Step 2: From the Big Picture to Value-added Actions. Use your understanding of what business you're in to create value-added actions.

Step 3: Value-Added Evaluation. Screen all your ideas to find the best, and most cost effective and the most appropriate.

VALUE ADDED IN LIFE INSURANCE

I've found that the big money-makers don't want to go to the doctor. They want the insurance, but it's just hard to get them to take the physical. So if they've bought enough insurance, I send a limo around to pick them up, take them to the appointment and then bring them back to their office afterwards.

ANN SPINAZZOLA, NorthWestern Mutual Life

VALUE-ADDED IDEAS

Besides the value-added process, Phase III salespeople add value in two areas that most salespeople miss. The first area concerns the relationship, what the one-to-one, face-to-face encounter looks like. Secondly, Phase III salespeople think and act in an entirely different manner when it comes to problems, foul-ups and irate clients. *What they do can only be called value added.*

INTERPERSONAL VALUE ADDED

One of the most powerful value-added experiences that you can create isn't related to product, service, or business problems. The most powerful of personal value-added experiences is making a difference in someone's life. Because your clients have met and dealt with you, they feel better about themselves. It's the unexpected, value-added gift of self-esteem. Think of a time that you dealt with someone who was 100 percent honest and 100 percent accountable. Someone who was involved with and cared about you on more than just a "ritual" level (the level of "Hi, how are ya, nice suit, nice tie, what's it going to take to close this deal?").

That kind of encounter made you feel pretty good, more important, more in touch with yourself and your self-worth. And people like that are few and far between.

So be that person with your clients. Give them that value-added experience. Much of what we've talked about in this book so far—purpose, intention and partnering—is about that kind of relationship. It's more work, it won't always happen—and some clients will reject it out of hand. But when it does come together, when it clicks, you've created something that is unique, special and very powerful.

VALUE ADDED IN SELLING AUTOMOBILE SERVICE

Think about the last time you brought your car in for service. Did you feel anxious? Did you not really trust the dealership to find and fix only what needed to be fixed? Sadly, those are normal expectations. And expectations that are easy for an Art Grayson to exceed.

Our goal is to be able to have our customers bring their cars in for service and all they have to say is "Do me." They will have total trust that we'll find and fix what needs to be fixed, not fix what doesn't need fixing. And they will trust us to make the judgment between the two. All for a fair price. When they come back for their car, it will be in perfect running condition. That's the kind of service we want to provide, that's the kind of relationship we want to have with our customers.

ART GRAYSON, Grayson Pontiac

Personal example of the interpersonal value added: I was twenty-five years old, selling life insurance, moderately successful. As anyone in the insurance business can and will tell you, prospects *always* have a million reasons why they don't need life insurance, won't buy life insurance and won't see a life insurance agent.

After dealing with at least half of those million reasons, I realized that they all basically came down to two common denominators: that the prospects didn't want to deal with the idea of their own death, and that they didn't have a sense of accountability to the ones they loved—for whatever reasons. Now, those are major issues, you don't just dive into them in the first meeting.

I worked on the problem of what business I was really in, what value-added actions I could take, and what would be the most effective way that, in a value-added way, I could really communicate about the larger issues. What I finally came up with was very simple, but effective.

At that time Earl Nightengale had a record called "The Strangest Secret." It was one of those rare works that in a very powerful and nonthreatening way dealt with deep issues like the purpose of life and the power of the self. It was very personal and meaningful. I decided to use the record. Once I had a confirmed appointment, I would send the record to the prospect with a letter confirming our appointment. A few days would pass. When I finally met with the prospect, the first question I would ask was, "How did you like Earl Nightengale's record?"

Then I would just listen. That simple recording had the ability to evoke a deep response from people. With many prospects, I would get into serious conversations about their basic fears, hopes and aspirations. We would discuss things that they had never voiced with a stranger before, things that many had not even discussed with their spouse. In those meetings, we never talked about insurance. But ultimately many of those people became my friends and clients.

What was the value added? Of course, giving prospects the record was part of it. But the real value added was interpersonal, it gave permission to prospects to see themselves in a different light. It helped them look at serious issues in their lives. We moved a relationship from ritual to meaningful. After those discussions, prospects felt clearer about what they wanted, and they planned to get it. They felt more in charge of their lives —and many times, buying life insurance became a natural extension of that feeling.

Helping people make personal decisions to improve their lives is the ultimate value added. And it's something that we all can give when we understand that our role is to be of service and to exceed the expectations of our clients even in terms of the relationship.

Phase III salespeople move the relationship from ritual to meaningful. A late, dear friend and colleague of mine, Bob Donoghue, had a phrase for this. He called it "love in the marketplace." It's the respect and caring between individuals. It's caring for the individuals whom we deal with, both personally and professionally —and being there to help. That's the essence of the value-added relationship.

VALUE ADDED IN FINANCIAL SERVICES

Paul Studebaker, of Criterion Financial Services in Minneapolis, is another master of the value-added relationship. I've known Paul for twenty years. He has gone from being our property and casualty agent to a full-fledged financial adviser on a number of matters involving financial risk. But what's different about Paul is the strength of his commitment and the warmth of his friendship. He acts as if my family were his family. He makes us feel as though we are his only clients—but Paul is a very successful businessperson. He has taken the insurance agent relationship and turned it into a relationship of nurturing care. It's clear that his purpose is to take care of us, not sell us insurance—and that's exceeding our expectations.

WHAT'S THE PROBLEM AND HOW CAN I HELP?

What do you do when there is a problem? When there is an angry and upset client? There are a couple of ways to think about it—but one way exceeds the expectations of clients.

"WHENEVER THERE'S A PROBLEM, I'M THERE"

Shinichi Yamamoto has sold cars for Mazda in a southern suburb of Tokyo for twenty-five years. For the past twenty years, he has always been one of the top salespeople for Mazda in Japan.

In Japan, selling automobiles is done differently from in the United States. When Yamamoto started, he would take the train twenty-five kilometers from his dealership and then walk back through the urban areas knocking on doors and making cold calls. His objective was to introduce himself and Mazda. That kind of dedication and work obviously paid off.

Today, as with Diane Flis of Buick, most of Shinichi Yamamoto's business comes from repeats and referrals. In fact, of the last three thousand cars that Yamamoto has sold, the majority have gone to the same eight hundred repeat clients. On average, that means he has sold close to three cars to each of his steady clients. Understand how Yamamoto thinks and works and you'll understand the loyalty he receives from his clients. And that's where value added comes into play.

Here's the story. Yamamoto had called on one prospect—who had never owned a car—a number of times. The man showed no inclination to buy a car, although he grew to know and trust Yamamoto. Finally, after a few months, the prospect came by the dealership, asked for Mr. Yamamoto, and told him that he was now ready to buy a car. After a demonstration and negotiations a car was selected and a contract signed.

That night, however, the new client's house and business burned to the ground. The following morning, as soon as Yamamoto heard about the fire, he rushed over to his prospect's house to help sift through the ashes and salvage what valuables had survived.

As Yamamoto puts it, at first his client was shocked when he saw his automobile salesman coming to his aid.

But as they cleaned together and sorted through belong-
ings, Yamamoto helped convince the man that he could
start again and rebuild his house and business. The
prospect was visibly touched. But with great loss of face
he asked Yamamoto to cancel the current order for the
Mazda. He then said that when he was reestablished
he would buy the car. Without hesitation, Yamamoto
agreed.

Here's the payoff. Within a year, the prospect rebuilt
his business—and he purchased the car. Since then,
that client has purchased over thirty vehicles—cars and
utility trucks—from Yamamoto, and he has sent all his
relatives to Yamamoto to buy Mazdas.

In Japan there is a tradition that loyalty, for example
that of a salesperson to a client, is very important and
it transcends the business relationship. What I have
learned is that one of the best ways to show my loyalty
is when a client is in trouble. When I find out about it, I
try to be there as soon as possible to help.

SHINICHI YAMAMOTO

Enormous opportunity exists when there is a problem,
when things are not going smoothly, even when clients
are angry—but you have to be thinking, you have to give
extra value.

Other Fires

There may not be a lot of real fires, but there will
always be those other fires; there will always be
glitches, screw-ups, overbillings and late deliveries.
Those are the cobras—the facts of an increasingly more
complicated landscape of business and selling. Given
that, our choice is whether we want to see opportunity
or crisis.

The size of the opportunity exists because nothing

bonds a client to a salesperson more than when a salesperson shows up after the sale, in the teeth of the gale,
and says, "I know there's a problem and it's not working
the way you expected. My job is to make sure you get
what you want."

PROBLEMS

*After the sale, it's our job to produce the product and
take care of problems. A lot of salespeople will back out
at that point, never to be heard from again. They got
their check, they're going to get their commissions at
some point—so they are history as far as that account
is concerned. It's like the great ad I heard on the radio
where the guy buys a personal computer from XYZ
shop, then he comes back in and the salesperson says,
"Do I know you?"*

*When I give people references, I always tell them to
find out, when they call the reference, how Alan Braslow is serving them after the sale—find out whether I
back up what I say, whether I go to their defense,
whether we screw something up. The nature of business
is that we will make mistakes. But where am I? Am I
there if you need me?*

*I'm going to be there on my client's side of the table
talking to our client's service people—and I'm going to
be standing up for the client because we're not producing what we should produce. They know that I am their
ombudsman.*

*The point is that you are morally obligated to take
care of the guy—and whatever problems or screw-ups
the guy has. Remember, that guy is sending your kids to
camp and paying your mortgage. Sure, you work for
your company, you're an employee and they pay you—
but the client is the one you really work for, and too
many in organizations forget that.*

ALAN BRASLOW, Five Technologies

"I'm your agent": that's exactly what I tell people. I'm on their side against the house, against the guy who runs the store.... It's important that they know that when they leave with that car, they know they can call me if they need anything. I tell people that I don't care whether it's just that they can't find the bathrooms in this dealership—by God, they better come to me and ask. They're what I'm here for, I'm their agent.

When I sell a car I tell the customer, "We'd all like to think that you won't have any problems with your car. But in case you do, our service area is our hospital. I want you to be familiar and comfortable with it." What's ironic is that the other salespeople—in a meeting last week—recommended never taking their prospects back to Service, because of the bad language they'd hear there and because they might see the same model car that they're considering with a problem. But it's a joke, because everybody knows that cars have problems and they sometimes need repairs. I think it's better to deal with it before it starts and make the people comfortable with the solution.

The point is that when you deal with people like this, they tell all their friends. They say, "Yeah, I had a problem, it wasn't a perfect car, but Diane got it handled for me." I'll take them back to the service adviser, even write up the order—I write up a lot of service orders.

DIANE FLIS, Buick

The next time you get the irate phone call, or hear that a client is not satisfied, instead of thinking, Oh, my God, how can I get out of this?, imagine that you were just handed a lead on a highly qualified prospect. Then, overwhelm the client with your accountability, support and commitment. Go out of your way to do whatever is necessary; be 100 percent dedicated to making sure that the problem is solved, that your client is more than satisfied. If you do that, the majority of the time you'll take a potential problem and turn it into an opportunity.

THE VALUE-ADDED TEAM

Valued added can play an important role in team sales and partnerships. As the leader of a sales team, and as the member of a partnership, one of your roles is the creating of a value-added team. This can be a subunit of the team, or even just one person whose mission is to keep asking and answering the question "How can we add value to this relationship and to this sale—how can we keep exceeding the expectations of the client?"

As the salesperson and the leader of the team, your task is to keep reinforcing value added. Act on the good ideas that your value-added team comes up with. Keep the entire team focused on adding value. Every day the question should come up, "How can we add value?" Make it the question with which you end every meeting. Make it part of the team culture. This kind of team thinking and a dedicated value-added team will have a huge payoff. It can't help but happen.

The other thing I do is go back to the service area every morning with the coffee. I might run into ten, twelve people back there who have their cars in for service. I look at their service order, talk to them about the problems they're having, buy them coffee and the like. Just being there for five minutes and showing that you care—they remember that.

But a lot of car salespeople say, "I'm not going back into the service department, man, those people are crazy back there. I'm not listening to those owners yell and scream. I might run into someone who's got a bad problem and they'll blame it on me. They'll think I sold them a bad car."

These guys are missing the boat.

Diane Flis, Buick

Recap

Value added begins with positive intention. Once your intention becomes to exceed expectations and to add value, you've just changed the game and you've changed your job. You've made what you do much more interesting and much larger in terms of its impact on your clients—and on yourself.

The final step is to use the ideas. Put them into action. Before every sales situation, every day, ask yourself, How can I add value? Make it the number-one question on your mental checklist.

After the sale, or the meeting—debrief. Ask, How did I add value? How did I exceed my client's expectations? What could I have done differently?

Take the time to review and critique; be your best advocate and critic. In the critiquing lies the real learning opportunity. That's the opportunity you have to really understand the power of Value Added.

It comes down to the fact that without value added, anybody could sell what you sell, could do what you do—including your competition. Value added is you making the difference. And if it is done right, no one will ever be able to compete against you.

THE MILLIKEN STORY
THE VALUE-ADDED COMPANY

Milliken and Company of Spartanburg, South Carolina, is a $2 billion textile manufacturer and one of our largest clients. As far as we are concerned, they are also one of the original torchbearers of value-added marketing. They are constantly teaching us at Wilson Learning what value added really means.

John Rampey, a Milliken officer, tells the story. Milliken began making giant strides toward becoming a value-added company in the late seventies. They were already known for being a premier manufacturing organization, but the organizational leadership made the decision to change the direction of the ship—to become more market driven and market focused.

One of the first decisions was to redefine the idea of quality to include not only the products, but all the services that were offered to their customers, including the service of marketing.

And this is where Milliken developed value-added marketing.

A large part of Milliken's apparel-customer base is made up of small companies that make clothing from Milliken materials. Small companies with small profit margins and limited resources in a rapidly changing, highly competitive industry.

The value-added questions that Milliken people asked themselves were: "How can we help our customers do a better job? How can we help them succeed and be more competitive?"

From those questions a host of innovative, value-added ideas came forth. For example, Milliken developed a "Partnering for Profit" program, under which it provided a variety of value-added services to its customers, one of which is a consulting service to help customers manage the manufacturing end of their businesses. Milliken provides service in everything from helping its clients decide on optimum widths and control sizes for orders to providing consulting help in the sewing rooms.

In this industry, cloth is made in batches and there

can be slight variations in color between batches that are very hard to discern with the naked eye. Not a serious problem, unless one leg of a pair of pants is made from one batch and the other leg from another batch. Milliken developed a system that it provides to its customers that allows them to measure and compare colors. Customers can manufacture a shirt in one plant and a pant in a different plant and then bring the sets together at a distribution center with confidence that the sets will match in color.

Another customer problem that Milliken identified was an information bottleneck. Its customers would order a product and get the product, but they would have to wait for the paperwork in order to know specifically what was on the loading dock, how much there was, and what to do with it. To solve this problem, the textile manufacturer started an electronic information network hooking up its customers to Milliken. Now customers have instant access to specific order information and billing information. Further, the company is working on a completely electronic order entry system. Milliken's huge database on apparel-marketing research is also available to its customers. Everything that Milliken knows about the retail market can be accessed by customers.

Beyond the Partners for Profit program, Milliken puts on quality-orientation workshops, in Spartanburg, for its customers' CEOs and COOs.

It's basically the same workshop that Milliken has put five thousand of its own employees through. Milliken will then assist customers in developing their own quality programs for their own people.

Milliken salespeople have all these value-added services at their disposal. But, more important, they have full permission and authority to continually be exceed-

ing the expectations of their customers. For example, if a Milliken customer has a materials-handling problem, a salesperson can bring in a Milliken materials-handling engineer to the customer site to suggest solutions.

Think of the competitive advantage. Customers having instant and easy access to product ordering and market information. Customers connected electronically to make it even easier. Customers and Milliken speaking and measuring quality out of the same hymnbook, using the same language. Customers coming to Milliken to solve business and manufacturing problems. Salespeople given virtually full permission to develop value-added solutions to help their customers be more successful.

That's the business strategy of purpose (helping others get what they want) and value added, coming from the top of an organization all the way out through the sales force to the customer.

Remember, value added is the Phase III competitive strategy.

Strategic Thought Process No. 6

Summary
Think: How can I exceed the expectations of my clients?

1. Step back and analyze your business. Look for the big picture. What do your clients really buy? What business are you really in?
2. Once you have your "big picture," create a list of value-added actions that exceed the real task and the personal expectations of your clients.
3. Evaluate your ideas. Put them through a cost/benefit fil-

ter. Which ones would have the highest impact? Give you the greatest positionable difference?

Value-Added Ideas:

Take the relationship beyond the ritual level. The most powerful of personal value-added experiences is making a difference in someone's life. Ask yourself, how can you make your clients feel better about themselves? Give the value-added gift of self-esteem.

Seek out problems. Nothing bonds a client to a salesperson more than the salesperson showing up after the sale when there is a problem, being 100 percent accountable and taking 100 percent responsibility for solving the problem. That exceeds expectations.

CHAPTER 11

STP NO. 7: APPLYING THE PRINCIPLE OF LEVERAGE

So far we've looked at innovation in selling, and what you could call the people side of selling. MBA's might call it "soft skills," but it's strategic thinking, innovation, partnering, leadership and value added that are changing the game of selling. The salespeople who religiously practice these STPs are the leaders in their industries—not only in production, but also in fulfillment and excitement. They will always be working in a world of abundance, because clients seek out innovators, partners and value-added leaders.

WHAT DOES THIS MEAN TO ME TODAY?

Now, if you got a memo on your desk today that said "Innovate, form partnerships, be a leader and add value," you'd probably think they'd have to add another three days to the week to make some of that possible. In a business world that's already complex and competitive, all that sounds like more work.

In order to assure that the Strategic Thought Processes aren't about *adding* more work, we need to spend a chapter being hard-nosed as we look at the business of selling in Phase III. How, amid increasing competition, increasing demands for our time and our energy, can we make all of this work?

I want to suggest a new way of working, a new game. For a number of years in selling, most of us kept working harder and harder, seeing prospect after prospect after prospect—an endless chain of one-shot sales, each one of them costing more time, more effort, with more competition than ever before. That's selling by the law of averages. See enough people and you're bound to make some sales.

GRAVEL AND GREASE

Clair Strommen, the chairman of the board of Lutheran Brotherhood, a Minneapolis-based Fraternal Life Insurance Company, tells a story about when he had his own agency. He had an agent who in one year made 3,000 calls, had 100 interviews and a fabulous volume. He had tripled his income. When Clair congratulated him, the agent responded, "That's great from your point of view, but I have had 2,900 rejections. Another year like that and I will be out of the business."

That is sometimes the result of the old game. The point, according to Clair, is that the traditional way of prospecting and the business of getting in front of potential buyers is very punishing. Clair draws the analogy that an agency is like the cogs and wheels in a machine. The old way of doing business is like forcing gravel through the machine. It eventually wears down all the parts. What is needed—and Clair has worked long, hard and successfully in this—is a system that adds grease to the machine instead of gravel.

And that is the goal of leverage: making the machine work smoothly, getting better results with less effort.

The new game is to discover ways of working effortlessly, getting the most done with the least amount of effort. It involves thinking like Tom Sawyer. With a little thought, a little strategic planning, you can get a bunch of people whitewashing your fence for you instead of standing out there in the hot sun doing it all by yourself.

THINKING GEOMETRICALLY

Applying the principle of leverage means finding ways to multiply our efforts, getting other people to help whitewash the fence. It's a way of thinking and acting, leveraging everything we do including our time and energy, every sale and every idea. It's moving from working harder to working smarter by following the laws of efficiency.

Leveraging is thinking geometrically rather than linearly. The result of linear thinking is calling on one prospect, running that sale out until completion and then starting completely over with a new prospect.

Thinking geometrically means establishing a strategic relationship with one highly qualified prospect and then, with recommendations and referrals, leveraging that first relationship into two other relationships, who recommend you to four other prospects, and so on. Much easier, much more efficient and thus more profitable than an endless series of cold calls.

From One Idea for a Speech . . .

Thinking geometrically means developing that one highly leverageable idea and then applying it, revising and adapting it to as many situations as possible.

For example, I started out with one speech—one idea —about selling. I leveraged that into a sales training course, Sales Sonics. With the help of a couple of key clients, that became Counselor Selling and then the Wilson Learning Corporation. Today, Wilson Learning Corporation is a $50 million-plus international company supplying over one hundred different applications of our counselor technology—and it all can be traced back to that one speech, to that one leverageable idea. That doesn't mean it didn't require a lot of time and energy from a lot of talented people. But the time and energy were spent, as an organization, leveraging a couple of ideas with a lot of potential.

THE LEVERAGE PRINCIPLE

Archimedes, the Greek mathematician and inventor, said, "Give me a rod that's long enough and a place to stand and I can move the earth." That's the essence of the principle of leverage: Achieve results with minimum effort by using the right tools. In selling, our tools are thinking strategically and thinking leverage.

Like value added, leveraging is an extra step that can pay off enormously. Like the question "How can I add value?" the question "How can I leverage this?" should become a daily ritual—it can become a natural part of your thinking process.

There are four ways that leveraging can play an important role. The first way we can leverage our time and energy is by working in the most efficient and effortless way; the second way is by prospecting; the third, by networking; the fourth, comes in after the sale.

LEVERAGE IDEA NO. 1: A PERSONAL STRATEGIC PLAN

John Wanamaker, the great Philadelphia retailer, once said that half of his advertising wasn't worth a damn—

the problem was he just didn't know which half. Knowing when we're effective and when we're not, and *how to be effective more of the time* is one of the easiest ways to leverage ourselves.

The 80/20 Rule

We discussed the 80/20 rule earlier: 80 percent of the sales are made by 20 percent of the sales force. Another application of that same rule is that usually 80 percent of your results come from 20 percent of what you do— 20 percent of your activity, 20 percent of your clients and even 20 percent of your thinking. In some cases this might be stretching the ratio. But no matter the size of the stretch, we want to spend most of our time doing our 20 percent. That means—even for the most disorganized among us—planning, prioritizing, and *letting go* of low-priority activities. We don't want to spend most of our time majoring in the minors. Our goal is to develop and stick to a personal strategic plan that allows us to be as productive as possible.

A Personal Leverage Audit

My friend Dick Leider, who works as a career and life planner in Minneapolis, tells his clients to give him their check register and their calendar and he'll tell them what their life priorities are. That's the first step in finding your 20 percent. Audit what you're already doing! Audit what you're spending your time and money on. If you have an administrative assistant, have him or her go through your calendar and give you a monthly activity report. Find out what you're paying attention to. What's illuminating about these kinds of audits is that we find that sometimes we tend to spend our time on what's comfortable (the known and the no-risk) instead of on what is effective, important and leveragable.

Try a Leverage Audit.
1. Start by making a list of all your activities. Everything from paperwork to strategizing, to client contact—everything in your work world that takes your time and energy.
2. Prioritize the list with these questions:
   a. What three things you do that bring in revenue?
   b. What are the things that a support person, a telemarketer for example, could do more efficiently than you? (Remember, if you figure your time is worth $50/hr and you can hire a support person for $15/hr, there might be a lot of things that you can let go of and save money at the same time.)
   c. Finally, what would you have to let go of—stop doing—in order to concentrate on the three things?
3. Act on the priorities! For the next two weeks, experiment—work only on those three things. Then analyze the experiment. Did you get more done? Do you feel better about what you did? Do you feel more in control? More productive? More "Phase III"?

Of course, we all have our quota of "annoyance" tasks, such as paperwork that has to be done. The goal is to not only minimize that kind of work, but also to be consciously aware of the priorities and the choices we have. In selling, especially as complexity increases and time becomes more valuable, everything we do needs to be put through a filter: Is this important? Is this on purpose? Is this my 20 percent? If not, why am I choosing to do it?

The Acid Test

The follow-up question, after you've got 20 percent is, Are you *doing* your 20 percent? Have you let go of or delegated all the activities that aren't part of your 20 percent? Almost always it comes down to the question, What are you willing to let go of, to get what you want? It's like throwing away the clothes in your closet that you haven't worn in six months. You have to stop doing what's not useful.

So keep asking the questions—post them on your mirror: "Am I working my 20 percent? Am I focusing on my three primary tasks?" Maximum results with the minimum effort—that's leverage.

GETTING LEVERAGE HELP

Sometimes leveraging your time and energy means doing unconventional things—getting help to take care of the 80 percent so that you can stay on top of the 20 percent.

One of the most exciting things that has happened to me was that I was able to sell my company the idea of my having an assistant. This was not an easy sale. There were a lot of political, emotional, psychological, financial and historical reasons why my company could have said no.

I had gone from the smallest territory with the least active brokers to the largest territory with the most active brokers. But I found myself spending way too much time in my office, tracking down files, answering the phone and doing paperwork. It was getting difficult to go out and see people. So we hired an assistant, I agreed to give her 5 percent of my commissions as a bonus, and it's been great. It has absolutely changed my working conditions and my ability to do what's really important, go out and be face to face with prospects and customers. This concept of teaming a salesperson with a full-time sales assistant is being viewed as a pilot program. If it works, it may be extended to other sales representatives.

KATHY MONTHEI, Delta Dental Plan of California

My office manager—a vital member of my team—suggested that I use a limo to drive to appointments. At first I was a little bit uncomfortable with the idea, but I decided to try it—and it has really helped. I can study, make my phone calls, listen to tapes; I can concentrate and not worry about driving. Before I got a limo and a driver I wasn't really using my time efficiently driving to appointments. This has really helped me be more productive, and it has really helped take the stress off.

ANN SPINAZZOLA, NorthWestern Mutual Life

LEVERAGE IDEA NO. 2: PROSPECTING: THE INVERTED FUNNEL

The old game of prospecting was thought of as a funnel. You put a lot of "suspects" in at the top, and, for that

FIGURE 7

Funnel Diagram

Suspects

Prospects

Qualified

Buyers

effort, out of the bottom you got those few highly qualified prospects who buy.

In this scenario the salesperson's job is to keep the top of the funnel full—activity-intensive prospecting. A lot of time and energy is spent, and, of course, most of the suspects that come in through the top never reached the buyer stage.

For example, the salespeople for one of our high-tech clients in Japan make up to one hundred cold calls a day. Knocking on doors, up and down the skyscrapers in Tokyo, trying to get that first appointment, trying to get suspects. That's an extreme, but it's based on the old "See more people" belief that confuses activity with accomplishment.

I'm going to suggest another model.

The Leverageable Prospect

Here's the principle. In addition to having the need for your product or service and having the resources to purchase your solution, the added criterion is that a prospect can *always* lead you to other business, either repeat or referral. The strategy then becomes not "How can I make this sale?" but instead, "How can I make this sale *and* how can this sale—or this relationship—lead me to other business?"

The corollary is: *Never* prospect for one-shot, one-sale business. Let go of it! It's simply not worth your time and energy. That sounds "ivory tower," especially if you're new to selling or new to a company, but it's the target you shoot for. Building a base of satisfied clients and then continually tapping into it is a Very High Business Priority.

Imagine what it would be like—even if you sell consumer goods—if you focused the majority of your time on clients who could lead you to other business. What would it be like if you spent your time following up on those clients, keeping those relationships going, instead of waiting for a new prospect to walk in the door or a new prospect list to come across your desk?

What this strategy needs is an up-front selection process to determine who your prospects are, a carefully thought-out strategy that takes you to the relationship you want—then follow through!

Try this: A model selection process to find leverageable prospects:

> Will my product or service solve a problem for them?
> Do they appear to have the financial resources necessary?
> Are they a good partnering prospect?
> If I establish a good relationship with them, can this lead to other business, regardless of whether I make this sale?

We're inverting the funnel. You have fewer, more qualified prospects at the top, but they are *prequalified* to bring you much more business at the bottom. Instead of activity-intensive prospecting, it's strategic-planning prospecting. Just like a strategically oriented organiza-

FIGURE 8

Inverting
the Funnel

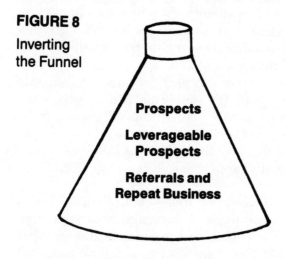

Prospects

Leverageable
Prospects

Referrals and
Repeat Business

tion, it's deciding in advance who your key accounts should be and then going to work, spending your time and energy—your 20 percent—pursuing those key accounts instead of just throwing out a net and seeing what you pull in.

When I began my real-estate career in '73–'74, we were experiencing the only recession that Atlanta has ever known. Since most corporations were curtailing relocating their people, the real-estate market was very slow. To keep busy, I decided to begin building my corporate clients instead of competing head on with other agents for in-town business, the way business is normally pursued. At the time, few agents were going after corporations and the relocation market. Once I was committed to that decision, my days were filled with cold calls to every major corporation I could think of all over the city. I remember calling on the Oldsmobile division of GM two dozen times before I received that first referral.

Now 95 percent of my business comes from corporate customers.

Eileen Tertocha, Skipper Morrison Realty

This is how Phase III salespeople think and work. They see far fewer people than is the norm for their companies or industries. But from each of their clients they get dramatically more production than is the norm, because they understand what their 20 percent is. They always get referrals, they always go for repeat business, and the old clients—established friends—are the first ones they go to with new ideas.

It's a chicken-and-egg situation. Because they see fewer clients, they have more time and resources to devote to their strategic clients—their partners—which results in more production, which allows them to continue to work with their partners, and so on. But somewhere for the game changers it starts with understanding that selling is not a numbers game, it's a productivity game.

It starts with letting go of the temptation to chase after the short-term, one-sale opportunities. Search for the business that can bring you more business; leave the rest to the salespeople playing the law-of-averages game.

Without referred leads I'm dead in the water. Because I work exclusively on referred leads. This means I get my clients' help in locating and contacting other clients. In other words, if a client doesn't tell me to call someone, I won't call them. I don't care how much money that other person makes or what they do. I have to be referred to them first. If someone calls in I know that one of my clients has referred me, because no one just looks up Ann Spinazzola in the Yellow Pages and says, "I believe I need some insurance today."

ANN SPINAZZOLA, NorthWestern Mutual Life

LEVERAGE IDEA NO. 3: THE LEVERAGED NETWORK

Building a network inside your client's organization, or with your client's associates and personal friends, is one of your first leveraging objectives once a relationship has been established.

By "a network" I mean getting to know as many people as possible—and having them get to know you. This is the internal referral process. A good network is composed of people across the organizational spectrum and especially up and down the chart. Remember, organizational charts are snapshots of a moving target. Especially in turbulent times, organization are being reorganized, people promoted, brought in or let go.

In a long-term relationship with a client, which is the goal, a lot of the individuals who appear far down on the organizational chart are actually moving up. They will be promoted to positions where they could help you or hurt you in five years, depending on whether they know you, like you and trust you.

FROM TOP OF THE CHART DOWN

In the sales cycle, an account manager deals with any number of individuals who are "unimportant" to the decision-making process. These people need information as much as anyone, but they aren't really crucial to the process—so it would be easy to ignore them. But it's important to remember that you're building a long-term relationship, and offending someone now could come back to haunt you later. The converse is also important: If you help those individuals now, they may be around to help you out somewhere down the line.

Charles Breckenridge, Cray Research

Every relationship is important, because you never know when you're going to meet these people later in your career. You may meet them at the first-line level right now, but in four or five years they might be middle management. Another ten years, they might be upper-middle management or higher. They may go from influencer to key decision-maker. It's so important to treat everyone with equal respect and courtesy. It's also important to have the same needs and problem-solving orientation with every client you meet.

Don Walker, Wilson Learning

Networking in Japan

A salesperson who thrives on his networking ability is Yoshitaka Suzuki of Nihon Electric Company (NEC) in Tokyo. He mainly works with only one client, a large securities firm in Tokyo. He began the relationship in 1978, when NEC was not doing much business with this corporation. Suzuki took this account from almost zero business to a constant $10 million annually. His entire approach is built on networking. As he puts it, his selling purpose is to increase the number of people who are his friends and the friends of NEC. At last count, Suzuki knew approximately three hundred individuals in various divisions and branch offices across his client's company. Just as importantly, those people know Suzuki and they associate him with information management solutions.

To listen to Suzuki describe how he networks is to hear it from a master. He started by getting to know one person, who at the time was relatively far down in the organization. After a few months, he sold that individual a small computer. With assistance from his "partner," Suzuki's computer helped make that person even more visible. As a result, Suzuki was introduced to other individuals who decided to use NEC, and so on. Soon Suzuki was working at the division level and introducing the president of NEC to the president of the client company. As he puts it, from that one sale of a small computer came the next one thousand sales—and the individual who was instrumental in that first computer sale is now a managing director and still a friend of Suzuki's; they came up the organizational chart together.

Currently, Suzuki's project is documenting his network and planning the next level of strategy. He's putting it all down on paper so that he can pass it on to the new account manager while he continues to move up in his client organization.

LEVERAGE IDEA NO. 4: AFTER THE SALE: REFERRALS AND REPEAT

Every sale you make, every problem you solve, every client who is ecstatic with what you've done is a leverageable opportunity. In most cases, it's after the sale—even after the client has used the product or service for a while—that the best opportunity exists for asking for repeat business and referrals.

But it takes two things. You have to call back, and you have to ask. When I speak to sales audiences about after the sale, I ask all those in the audience who call clients back religiously after every sale to raise their hands. Usually 5 to 10 percent of the audience raise their hands. So I ask, why don't more salespeople make the phone call or the personal appearance after a sale? The consensus of the groups almost always is that there might be a problem. The product or service that was purchased might not be meeting expectations. And no one wants to get into the middle of a problem.

That belief is enough to stop a lot of salespeople from even picking up the phone, and that's a great opportunity missed.

I've Got a Problem and I Need Your Help

The best opportunity in the world to ask for help is when you've just provided help to someone else. Whether you've sold the perfect solution or you've come in after the sale, with 100 percent commitment and 100 percent accountability, and taken care of client and the firestorm, that's the best opportunity you'll ever have to ask for help. It's simple, it's powerful and it's reliable. People want to help people who help them. But you have to help the client, and then you have to ask!

How Salespeople Get Paid

Next, understand that the way we get paid for our work isn't just in money—it's in referrals and in repeat business. Every sale you make is worth more to you than just that sale. Back in the early sixties, I used to put on open seminars all over the country, and I'd work hard to get those seminars filled. But each of the individuals that attended the open seminars meant more to me than just a sale. If I did my job right, if I exceeded their expectations, those individuals were all gateways to new business and new opportunities. I would mentally put a dollar figure on the repeat or referral business potential that each participant represented. It helped me keep my attention focused, and it motivated me to always ask. Again, when you help people, people want to return the favor—provided that you ask.

REPEAT BUSINESS: THE RESULT

When people come back to buy a car for the second time, you can skip a lot of the who-I-am and who-you-are type of things—they already know you and trust you. And I've got a pretty good idea of what color they like, what equipment was on their last car, and I know what they're going to use the car for. And I even call people up and say, "You know, this new car is right up your alley. I think you'll really enjoy this. Why don't you stop by when you get a minute, we'll take one for a drive." The point is they know me and they trust me. I even sent a guy a catalogue the other day, and I said, "Just like Saks, Sears, and Bonwit, here is your new '86 Buick catalogue. Come in and order your new Park Avenue, because I know you need one by January first." I got five orders from his company for cars.

DIANE FLIS, Buick

HIGH-LEVEL LEVERAGING

The Entrepreneur: Does This Idea Have GLO?

Let me introduce you to Walter Hailey, from Mesquite, Texas. Walter is one of my longtime friends. We both started in the insurance business and both struck off on our own at about the same time. Walter is a five-foot-six walking, talking embodiment of the leverage Strategic Thought Process.

I first met Walter back in 1964 when I was on the speakers' circuit. Whenever I was in the Southeast Walter would come to my speech, and he would always buy ten or fifteen copies of the book I used to sell. One day I asked him what he did with the books, and he told me that he gave them away. That tells you a bit about Walter.

At that time Walter worked for a little insurance company called Lone Star Life. One of the reasons I enjoy Walter so much is that he fulfilled the dream of every salesperson I've ever known. One day, he got so mad at the company that he walked in and bought the company —lock, stock and policies.

Then, about ten years ago, Walter sold that same company to K Mart for $78 million. *Now* you want to hear more about Walter Hailey, right? I asked Walter once when he became a millionaire. He said when he was seventeen—it just took a little while for the money to show up.

Walter's gift, besides being bright and articulate— and, Walter would add, Texan—is that he understands and uses leverage at the idea level. Whatever the idea, Walter always asks these questions: "Does this idea have GLO—generalized leverageable opportunity? How can this be leveraged? Who else can use this?" Walter's master strategy is to find the large opportunities, develop a solution and then refine the solution until it is easy to understand and sell. Then he moves it into the marketplace, living with it and selling it until the market is saturated. Only then will he move on to the next leverageable idea.

Walter leverages ideas. His 20 percent is looking for ideas with a high leverageability quotient, with a lot of GLO.

For example, he created a package of insurance products for the retail grocery industry, and he brought the grocery store owners together into an insurance pool as partners to share the risk. Then he replicated the same formula all over the country.

He also is a master at leveraging relationships. Walter used to call on a lot of CEOs of major companies in the Southwest. And he always used to run into the problem "Who is this little guy from Mesquite, Texas?" It was tough to get that first appointment.

At the time, one of Walter's friends was Bud Wilkinson, the coach of the University of Oklahoma football team. Bud was a national sports figure and the closest thing to a deity in that part of the country. Walter went into business with Bud. He would call up a CEO and say that Bud Wilkinson wanted to see him, and incidentally Walter Hailey was going to come along. That was an offer that most CEOs found hard to refuse. Once they got in the door, of course, Walter and Bud went to work. But it was Bud Wilkinson and Walter's ability to leverage a relationship that started the ball rolling.

An important postscript. What is so typical of Walter is that not only did he leverage his relationship with Bud, but at the same time he helped Bud Wilkinson leverage his ability and fame into financial success. Bud needed Walter as much as Walter needed Bud. Leveraging works best when it is a mutually beneficial partnership.

NEER

Naturally existing economic relationships: This is what Walter looks for. It isn't "Whom else do you know who has a similar problem I can solve?" Instead, it's "Who has a naturally existing relationship with someone who has a problem that our expertise could solve—a relationship through which we *can buy for them*, instead of selling the solution to them?"

For example, Walter's personal doctor, David Mc-Mahon, was having a problem with malpractice insurance because the rates kept going up so fast. He asked Walter for a solution. Walter and his associate, Jack Murphy, put together an insurance-buying company for the doctors of Texas. They started in Texas and then leveraged the idea through the doctors to other states. They now have eighteen thousand doctors served in forty states, and the company—which buys malpractice insurance for its clients—is growing by leaps and bounds. The public company is now called the American Physicians Service Company.

Walter and his partners have used this same concept —leveraging naturally existing economic relationships —in eight different industries and have made several hundred million dollars. That's the beauty of NEER.

Try this: Analyze ideas for Leverageability:

> Who needs your idea and knows it? Whom do you already know who would be interested in this idea? What relationships do you already have that could help you get your idea in front of the right people?
>
> What are the natural economic relationships that exist? What economic relationships do you have that you could tap into? Who are your client's clients? How could you add value to your client's relationships with his clients? How could you reduce costs or add value for those clients?

ALWAYS THINK LEVERAGE

As business becomes more complex, as your time becomes more expensive to you and more valuable to your clients, leveraging will be the key to help you multiply your efforts. To make it work, you need to expand how you think.

Always be asking, How can I leverage this? Who else can benefit? Who else needs to know about this idea?

Next, always ask for referrals and recommendations. A satisfied client is leverage that is waiting for you to call back. *Consider it sacrilegious not to.* Ask your best clients to recommend you, ask them to make phone calls and write letters for you. Remember Tom Sawyer—ask your clients to help you whitewash the fence.

Finally, be very careful about spending your time on business that has no leverageability. Focus on your 20 percent. No sale, no idea, no business relationship should pass by you without going through the leverage filter.

Thinking leverage is a discipline and, like value added, one that has enormous payback potential. It takes practice to become habit. Once leverage is habit, you've started to work smarter instead of harder.

Strategic Thought Process No. 7

Summary
Think: How can I leverage this?

Leveraging means using the right tools to get the most done with the least amount of effort.

1. Eighty percent of your results come from 20 percent of your efforts. Prioritize your activity, discover your 20 percent. Then stick to it, work your 20 percent. Let go of the 80 percent. Don't confuse activity with accomplishment.
2. Call only on prospects with high leverageability:
   A high probability for repeat business.
   A high probability for referrals and personal recommendations.
   Resist one-shot, one-sale opportunities.

3. Develop a network inside your client's organization. Develop a broad base of support. Look for new internal clients.
4. After the sale, always call back, always ask for referrals and personal recommendations.
5. Evaluate your ideas for GLO (generalized leverageable opportunity) and NEER (naturally existing economic relationships). Put them through a leverage filter:

   Who needs your idea and knows he or she needs it?
   Whom do you already know who would be interested in this idea?
   What relationships do you already have that could help you get your idea in front of the right people?
   Who needs your idea but doesn't know it?
   What are the natural economic relationships that exist?
   Who economically influences whom?
   How could you tap into that relationship?

6. Always think leverage! Always be asking, How can I leverage this? Who else needs this idea? Who else can benefit?

PART III

WOMEN, MANAGERS, AND THE NEW GAME

In this final section we need to look at the implications of the transformation of selling for two very special audiences—saleswomen and sales managers.

One of the most important demographic factors of the last thirty years has been the entrance of women in large numbers into the work force. It's changing the nature, the scope and the very purpose of business. Yet many women still feel trapped in dead-end jobs and feel that they are not a part of the dramatic changes occurring in our economy. Selling, as a career choice, could be the option that changes that for a lot of women. Many women have already discovered this, and they are making their mark on the profession. The title of Chapter 12, The Natural Superiority of Women, is taken from the landmark book by the anthropologist Ashley Montagu. In that chapter we will look at the natural abilities that women bring to selling, especially in the relationship area, and we'll look at what selling in the future can offer career-oriented women.

As for sales managers, managing Phase III salespeople will be a new job. The old ways, increasingly, won't work—the old ways being: hiring a lot of people to see who survives, managing autocratically, and not understanding how to develop salespeople.

Phase III will require a completely new set of strategies and responses in order to create, manage and nurture the high-performing sales team.

CHAPTER 12

THE NATURAL SUPERIORITY OF WOMEN

If I were asked . . . to what the singular prosperity and growing strength of that people ought mainly to be attributed, I should reply: to the superiority of their women.
    —ALEXIS DE TOCQUEVILLE, *Democracy in America,*
                                                    1840

I was a teacher. I taught home economics, family living—that sort of thing. I was single and I was having a little bit of a problem making ends meet. So I thought, what could I do that I would enjoy, on weekends and evenings, to supplement my income—I really wanted to keep on teaching, because I loved it. A friend of mine suggested trying the insurance business. I thought that would probably be a little bit easier than being a waitress or working in a department store. Nobody grows up thinking he or she wants to be an insurance salesperson. At the time, I really didn't think how much I'd really be helping people. I was thinking about making more money. After some research, it was clear to me that NorthWestern Mutual Life was the company to be with if you wanted the best. So I went with them, did my research and got my license.

The first two days of working I still had my teaching job, because, remember, this was only going to be part-time work. Anyway, the first two days of selling I made $1,000 each day. Now, I was coming from a twelve-month contract, head of the department, but making only $15,000 a year! After those first two days, I marched in, resigned and said, "I'm going to sell full time."

Ann Spinazzola, NorthWestern Mutual Life

This chapter is about women in selling. Specifically it is written for women seeking a career that, in general, has much greater earning potential than most, more freedom and, finally, a career that rewards strictly on the basis of performance. No other profession in our economy rewards performance better than selling, and, ironically, no other profession is in such dire need of the natural talents that women bring to the marketplace.

This is especially true as we look at the future of business five and ten years from now. Selling is going to be an even more visible and rewarded career. Most excellent organizations already understand that one of their greatest resources is their salespeople. It's the marketing force, the people out in the field, who are in touch with what clients want—now and in the future. Even companies that are less than excellent—the ones that always thought of their sales force as an encumbrance rather than a resource—are waking up and understanding the importance of salespeople. In the next ten years, selling is going to be the place to be. Organizations will spend the time and the money to develop salespeople, and sales career paths will point right to the top of most organizations.

Believe me, this is not the way it's been—but this is the way that it will have to be for companies to survive the shift to Phase III. When survival means staying close to your clients, it won't be the MBA's who have the skills. It will be the people who have lived and worked "staying close" that are going to run companies. In fact, as I see the future, it's quite possible that in ten years the norm will be that *selling experience will be a prerequisite* for any kind of upper-management position. Tom Peters and Nancy Austin, in their book *Passion for Excellence*, see this trend as critical to the pursuit of excellence for companies. In their examination of highly customer-focused companies they claim that "salespeople fill, even dominate the top executive ranks . . . a minimum of 50 percent of, say, the top fifty managers have spent a substantial share of their careers in selling."

It's clear to me that selling, more than ever before, is where the action, excitement and opportunity are. And this is especially true for women.

THE LONG MARCH FROM THE SMOKE-FILLED CONVENTION HALL

A little history. I've spoken to thousands of sales groups. Up until the late seventies, most sales audiences were made up of a sea of male faces. In audiences of sometimes a hundred salespeople, there would be only one or two women. Many people believed (and some still do) that selling was uniquely an undertaking for men. The characteristics of the high-performing salesperson were "masculine"—competitive, tough, a gunslinger. It was a men's club, a world in which women didn't play a major role.

To say that things are changing—and have changed—

is an understatement. To give you one isolated example of the rapidity and size of the change: As I'm writing this, in the summer of 1986, four of the top five, and eight of the top ten salespeople at Wilson Learning are women. Forty percent of that company—up and down the organizational chart—are women.

We would love to take credit for this, but all we did was hire people who were great performers and who fit into our culture. The fact of the matter is that the economy is being changed to its roots by the increasing number of women in the marketplace.

It's a fundamental change and a great blessing.

WOMEN AS CUSTOMERS

One of the changes that is forcing a lot of companies to change their ways is the fact that there are more women customers—with more economic power—than ever before. This is true both at the corporate level and in the consumer markets. Companies in every industry are figuring out that women customers are not going to buy from companies that appear to be exclusive male clubs. Many companies are scrambling to redress the imbalance and understand what, how and why women buy. Women in selling will play a large role in that educational process.

WOMEN AND BUYING POWER

A recent study showed that women make 80 percent of the buying decisions, whether it's on their own or involved in a partnership with a husband or a counselor of some sort. The study also determined that this is a huge dollar market that's being lost in the automobile industry every year.

Women are working their own jobs, making their own

*money, buying their own cars for business and to drive
the kids to school—it's their car, they're going to make
the decisions. Women are definitely more well read.
They research financing, the type of car, the mechanical
aspects of it. They're not just interested in trim and
color—that's a thing of the past.*

*But there is still a lot of misunderstanding of these
changes. For example, I bought my house when I was
twenty-three years old. I had a sizable down payment
ready and I could afford to pay $1,000 a month. At the
time, that put me in a real heavy market. I drove up to
a development in a brand-new Buick, I dressed in $300
cowboy boots, a nice pair of Levi's, a crisp shirt and a
down vest; it's Saturday, my day off, I'm not going to
dress up. I couldn't get people to pay attention to me
and show me houses. It was "Bring your husband back"
and "Where's your mom and dad?" They said things
like "The models are open. If you see something you
like, let us know." I was appalled. I ended up buying a
house through a builder. It blows my mind. It's unbe-
lievable the amount of prequalifying that goes on.*

DIANE FLIS, Buick

The demographics of the marketplace are changing;
there will be no "male sanctuaries" left. Women are
playing and will increasingly play a large role in management, in selling, and in creating the basic values of
corporations and of the marketplace.

*It worries me a lot that even though there are a few
of us selling now, there should be more. . . . I think there
is a lot of wasted potential out there. And the opportunity is so great. For example, the number-two woman at
NorthWestern Mutual Life in 1984 was Marion Mc-
Geary; she sold somewhere around $10 million and
she's been in the business only a year and a half. So the*

*potential is there. I think a lot of women are not letting
themselves have permission to do it, to go for it.*
ANN SPINAZZOLA, NorthWestern Mutual Life

IN MY OWN BACKYARD ...

I also have personal bias. I have four adult daughters
and a daughter-in-law all in business together. Two are
in selling—one with a corporate background and one
out of retail—and three are in management. From the
perspective of a father, I've watched them work hard,
run into the male bureaucracy, persevere and make it.

It's what my daughters have done recently—together
—that has taught me more about the potential of women
in business than anything else that has happened in my
professional life. The five of them have come together
from different areas of the country and different backgrounds to manage and run our Pecos River Learning
Center.

I came into this venture "on automatic," thinking that
maybe I should hire a president, who would be a man,
of course. But these women took over, created the vision, worked together as a team, built the organization,
supported each other and created a viable business
where most veteran businesspeople would have shaken
their heads and said the whole thing was impossible.

So if I needed any more converting, the last two years
of watching and participating with those five women
have done it. Women are and will be a powerful force in
the marketplace—and it's happening none too soon.

THREE REASONS WHY YOU SHOULD CONSIDER SELLING AS A CAREER

Back to the issue at hand. Why should a woman consider a career in selling? I'm going to throw out three reasons.

1. You Have Natural Talents

The first reason has to do with talents that are naturally feminine, and how these natural talents impact on selling. To begin with, think of the shifts in selling that have been described in this book:

From competitive to cooperative.
From adversarial to partnerships.
From short-term to long-term relationships.
From "Lone Rangers" to teams.

A lot of these changes are shifts toward what are generally recognized and reinforced in our culture as feminine abilities. Women tend to have a more cooperative viewpoint, and they tend to be more patient than men and, in general, to be more sensitive to relationships.

Yes, those are generalizations. Of course there are women who are competitive as hell and there are men who are incredibly patient. But in general terms there are differences between the ways men and women approach these very basic issues. The issue is not women versus men, or femininity versus masculinity. It's simply that women in our society have been reinforced throughout our cultural history for developing certain abilities. Those abilities just happen to be what is needed to be successful in selling today.

THE ANTHROPOLOGIST'S VIEW

*Women acquire ... a competence in social under-
standing which is usually denied the male. The female's
... practice of the art of human relations continues
throughout life; and this is one of the additional reasons that enable women to perceive the nuances and
pick up the subliminal signs in human behavior which
men usually fail to perceive ... they do not think in
terms of black and white, yes and no, or in terms of the
all-or-none principle, as men are inclined to do....
Women are more ready to make adjustments, to consider the alternative possibilities, and to see the other
colors and gradations in the range between black and
white.*

ASHLEY MONTAGU, the anthropologist, in *The
Natural Superiority of Women*

Peggy Steele, a Denver-based training consultant,
says it this way: "One of the things that I've observed is
that men in selling usually invent techniques for relating—memorize questions to ask or things to say in order
to move the relationship along. For women, it seems to
come much more naturally—it seems easier for women
to simply relate, to self-disclose and to talk about feelings—which, bottom line, has an enormous amount to
do with where the sale goes."

For many women, Phase III selling abilities will
come naturally. Not that there won't be any learning
involved, or any work, but to a great extent the "people
skills" foundation will already be in place. The talent
will be there.

*I definitely feel that I bring a very feminine compo-
nent to what I do. It's a different style. And it's clear to
me that if I tried to put that away someplace and save*

it for the weekend, it would limit what I do. I just have this sense that I love to listen to people, to find out what they're thinking and feeling about their life on a very real level.

That's what I love about my job—relating with clients and with people from my company.

I have this ability, I guess, to disclose—to reveal things—about myself. That somehow gives permission to the other person to disclose things about themselves at a deeper level. Within the context of that kind of relationship, all sorts of things become possible in terms of doing business.

Now I don't know whether it's just that most men don't operate comfortably at that level, or whether it's that a lot of people don't operate at that level. But it's my suspicion that in this day and age it's a feminine quality.

KATHY MONTHEI, Delta Dental Plan of California

It's important to add this note. Selling is not inherently a masculine or a feminine career. Those kinds of distinctions are prejudices. The facts of the matter are that we all have—no matter what sex we are—the abilities that are labeled, probably inappropriately, as feminine. We all have the ability to be intuitive, patient, sensitive to the nuances of relationships and open to all the options that exist between black and white. Some of us simply need to work harder than others at developing those natural abilities.

2. You'd Be Paid for Productivity

"Pay me what I'm worth." Does that sound like a familiar thought? If it does, and you think that you're not being paid what you're worth, remember this: Selling—in almost every industry and organization—is unique in terms of how people are compensated. More than in any other profession, compensation is linked to talent and productivity, not to less relevant, more bureaucratic indicators. Productivity is the way score is kept in selling. It doesn't matter how long you've been with the company, what your previous work experience was or whether you show up at work every day. You don't get paid for any of those; you get paid for producing. If you don't produce, you don't get paid. The more you contribute, the more you make. It's direct, immediate and easy to measure.

Further, academic credentials or impressive resumés don't really count for much. Look at the women you've met in this book. They are some of the highest performers in their industries. But they all come from very diverse, non–business-oriented backgrounds. Eileen Tertocha was a singer with a degree in music education. Kathy Monthei was the assistant executive director for the Oakland Educational Association, Diane Flis demonstrated mobile homes, Ann Spinazzola was a schoolteacher. Not exactly Harvard Business School resumés. In fact, not many companies would have hired them and promoted them in areas other than selling, because they lacked the "right" credentials. Now they are all highly successful, highly respected saleswomen. Because they grabbed an opportunity, they produced, and that's the only yardstick that counts in selling. Not many other professions can make that claim.

3. You'd Have Freedom

Selling is the closest you can get to having the freedom of being self-employed and still having a job. And more autonomy and more freedom are on the way as a result of authority being pushed down through organizations, and of companies waking up to the value of their salespeople. For a lot of companies, the model of the

salesperson will be the independent businessperson—
with the company behind her to act as a resource and as
a support team.

THE CLOSE

Time to summarize and close this "recruiting" pitch.
If you're a woman, if you're ambitious or if you
feel constrained by your current work situation, think
about making a career change. With most of the best
companies, selling offers more freedom than any
other occupation, you're paid for productivity and it's
a career that uses natural feminine abilities. That's
quite an attractive package. The icing on the cake is
that selling is where the future in business is. The
best salespeople, those individuals who really understand what the business is all about, are the ones
who will be targeted toward the tops of the organization charts.

Of course there will be exceptions—there will always
be those few companies that treat their sales forces like
the enemy and hire women only because the government says they have to. But they will be increasingly in
the minority and you will read about their business failures in the newspapers. For the rest of the marketplace,
the future of selling is brighter than it has ever been and
the opportunities for women in selling are just beginning.

So if you're a woman, think about it. Weigh the options. Look at your present job. Are you underemployed? Is your career path blocked? If you're in an
organization you like but in a job you don't like, maybe
it's time for a move sidewise before you can move up—
by applying for a job in selling.

If you're looking for a new company, or a new career,
find one of those companies that understand the future

and understand the importance of their salespeople. When you find the right company, beat its doors down to start a career in selling.

"The Natural Superiority of Women" Summary

For women considering new careers, or a career move, selling offers excellent opportunities for three reasons:

1. The natural abilities of women match up with how selling is changing:

   From competitive to cooperative.
   From adversarial to partnerships.
   From short-term to long-term relationships.
   From "Lone Rangers" to teams.

A lot of these changes are shifts toward what are generally recognized and reinforced in our culture as feminine abilities.

The next two reasons why selling could be the right career choice for women stem from the fact that many women tend to be underemployed—their abilities and talents are not being fully utilized and they are not being paid what they are worth.

2. Selling, more than any other profession, links compensation to talent and productivity. Productivity is the way score is kept in selling. The more you contribute, the more you get paid.

3. There is more freedom in selling, more opportunity to be self-managed and self-motivated than in most careers.

CHAPTER 13

MANAGING THE HIGH PERFORMANCE SALES TEAM

What can sales managers do to help their people grow, to help them thrive as Phase III salespeople? How can sales managers respond to rapidly increasing competition—not only competition for clients, but also increasing competition for the best salespeople?

THE SALES MANAGER'S ROLE

Mary Nygaard is a new, very talented sales and marketing manager in a new division of a new company: US West. US West, a regional holding company, is a creation of the AT&T divestiture. It's a Fortune 500 telecommunications company that is made up of twenty-two subsidiaries doing business in fourteen Western and Midwestern states.

Mary's organization is US West Materiels Resources. They provide procurement contracts, materials, management and reclamation services to twenty-two US West subsidiaries (for example, Northwestern Bell,

261

262 / CHANGING THE GAME

Mountain Bell and New Vector Inc.). It's a $1 billion-plus market, of which Mary's division owns approximately a 25 percent share.

Mary's situation and opportunity illustrate the changes that most sales managers today are experiencing. They're also a very accurate example of what is going on in all the old AT&T companies at the marketing and sales level.

Mary has two sales managers and ten salespeople working for her, all hard-working, talented and dedicated—and none of them with any major previous sales experience. All are Phase I salespeople who moved into selling from the old organization. Of course, complicating that even further is that the US West culture is in transition from an internally focused government-regulated "Bell-shaped-heads" organization to a market-focused organization in a very competitive environment.

New people and an exponential increase in competition (from none to competing with every wholesale supplier and management consultant in the West)—sound familiar?

Of course it doesn't end there. In what is really this group's start-up year, Mary's Phase I salespeople are being asked to quickly learn Phase III selling skills. Her level-one managers and salespeople need to call on the CEOs of the subsidiaries. They need to understand how to partner and to leverage those relationships into sales with the other subsidiaries. They also have to understand and relate to other former AT&T customers who are going through the same kind of turmoil that they're experiencing.

The sales managers, besides having to learn a new, higher-level sales process, must learn coaching skills, how to reinforce their people and keep them motivated through a long learning curve. They must also learn how to hang on to their good people—because the pool of talented salespeople is rapidly shrinking.

Training, supporting, hiring, keeping on top of quotas, helping people learn brand-new, higher-level skills in order to work in a higher-level market, and at the same time keeping the business going while everything is changing—that's the job description for a sales manager at US West.

And it's probably a fairly accurate job description for sales managers everywhere, as the game of selling creates a new game of sales management.

To better understand the new game of sales management, we need to first shift our thinking about what the job really is. Then I'm going to review the five factors—researched by Wilson Learning over the last ten years—that are critical to producing the high-performing sales teams that are the goal of most managers.

THE SHIFT: WHY MANAGING WITH THE GUN DOESN'T WORK

Not long ago, I watched the completion of one of the finest sales successes I had seen in a long time. The product was an expensive piece of educational software. From beginning to end the total sales cycle took more than twelve months to complete. The salesperson was the VP for sales of a small software company. He did everything right. He developed the appropriate strategy, he appealed to the correct motives of his buyers, made an on-target presentation and closed the sale.

But the next day I watched this same obviously talented sales VP conduct his weekly sales meeting. It was as if all his people sensitivity and competence were forgotten. He dominated; he pushed his solutions and ideas on his staff, seldom asking for their reactions or ideas. Through my eyes, it was clear that he didn't make a single sale that day—but he wasn't even aware of the

lack of buy-in from his staff. It was also clear that he
didn't believe that he was in the room to make a sale.

Why didn't he use the interpersonal skills he obviously had when it came to dealing with his own salespeople? My conclusion was that he didn't use them
because he didn't think he had to use them.

For many managers, this is a very easy trap to fall into.
We can be pretty good with people skills when dealing
with clients, because we realize that when we're selling
we don't have *control*, only *influence*. Unfortunately,
when we turn to face our employees, we stop being
marketers and try to be bosses. We think we control our
people. We think we pay them to do what they're told
and we have the power to fire them if they don't. An
illusion that gets us into a lot of trouble.

The Willy Sutton School of Management

Willy Sutton said it best. Willy was one of the world's
great management strategists. He was also one of the
world's greatest bank robbers. Willy's management philosophy: "You can influence more people and get further with a kind word and a gun than you can with a
kind word alone." Managing with the gun has been the
way we've traditionally managed and controlled people.
It was "Do it my way or else."

But one of the fundamental changes in management
today is that managers—from CEOs to sales managers—
no longer have the gun, because the gun is being shared.
More people have a piece of it, the right to say no, the
right to dispute, the right to do what they want to do.

And you haven't seen anything yet.

THE FUTURE: NOT ENOUGH QUALIFIED SALESPEOPLE

*The Bureau of Labor Statistics projects that from
1984 to 1990 the number of workers in the 16–24 age*

bracket will decrease by 2.7 million to 21.3 million; from 1990 to 1995 the group is expected to drop by another 1.1 million. . . . eventually the impact of this labor shortfall is bound to spread. Warns Walter Cadette, a Vice President and economist at Morgan Guaranty Trust, "McDonalds' and Burger King's shortages today will be GM's and IBM's tomorrow."

TIME magazine, April 28, 1986

A decrease in the number of qualified workers, plus an increase in the complexity and sophistication of selling should be a red flag to all sales managers. It signals an era of increasing competition for the best and the brightest.

The best and the brightest are going to be heavily recruited and, therefore they are going to have a whole lot more to say about whom they want to work for and what they want to do. To sales managers of the future, that's simply one more indication that managing with the gun won't work. Another strategy is needed. If we want to hire and retain the most committed work force possible and change the behavior of our salespeople, the first step is changing our behavior and overcoming the illusion that we can control them—that we can manage with a gun.

INFLUENCE AND PERSONAL POWER

Our executive committee understands that control doesn't work, so we don't have a lot of policies at Cray. We trust our people to use their best judgment. Our people are smart, with a lot of integrity, intelligence and initiative, and they're going to do the right thing if given the chance. The only real power we have to influence our people, then, is personal power. The way we gain our people's respect and cooperation is through that personal power, which comes from our setting an

*example and our knowledge of the business. None of us
are hung up on wanting to have more organization or
more control. We're convinced that that doesn't work.*
MARCELO GUMUCIO, executive vice-president for
marketing, Cray Research

Selling Careers

Peter Drucker said it all when he wrote, "The business of business today is selling careers." As sales managers, what we want, especially as competition increases and business becomes more complex, is the best and most committed people available. That's not something we can control, but that is something we can influence.

WHO ARE YOUR CLIENTS?

Go to work tomorrow imagining that you have two groups of clients. One is the group you already know: the people who buy your products and services. The other group of clients is the people who work for you. As managers, we need to learn how to sell a process called "work" to those people—that's the other business we're in. We need to sell work in the same manner we sell our product and services. Just as you ask yourself about your clients, ask yourself, How good is the relationship I have with my clients/salespeople? What do they really want and need? How can I best fit what I have to offer with what they need? How can I get them to make a commitment? Those are marketing questions. That's how we need to think when we're thinking about our employees.

From Coasting to Committed

What do we really want from salespeople? What are we trying to influence them to buy? When it's all boiled down, what we want is optimum performance, which means *people giving their best effort working on the right things.* Usually, as managers, getting people to work on the right things is something we have a direct influence on. But what about the best-effort factor? We do have the right to fire people, but most people have developed the survival skills to achieve at least a four out of ten—they know how to safely coast.

What about the idea that you pay people to perform? It means that we think we're paying them whether they perform optimally or not. What we are getting is the effort *they choose to give us* on a scale from four to ten. Four to seven is what we might term a compliance effort. Eight to ten is what we call a committed effort. As sales managers, most of us expect total commitment from our sales force. In reality, we're lucky when we're getting midrange compliance.

GETTING TO TEN: THE HIGH-PERFORMANCE WORK TEAM

We've done a considerable amount of research on the factors that contribute to moving people into the eight-to-ten range, the committed-effort range. We call that a high-performing work team. We define such a team as *"a group of committed people who, by working and sharing together, are getting optimal results over a long period of time because they are doing what they want to do and being who they want to be."*

The Work Culture

The work culture is the key to high performance. After surveying thousands of work units (a work unit is made up of a peer group of workers plus their immediate boss and their boss's boss) we've learned that the culture is very good at predicting the work unit's performance level.

More important, influencing the work culture is a manager's best opportunity for creating high performance. "Culture" is a twenty-four-hours-a-day training program that exists inside any organization. It's teaching and influencing all the time. Sometimes it's teaching what we like it to teach, and sometimes it's not. It's very difficult to "swim upstream" against the culture. For example, you can teach value added and long-term relationships all you want, but if the work culture is *really* about short-term, adversarial relationships with clients, that's what you're going to get—that plus a lot of confusion.

The best of all possible worlds is a consistent, positive, reinforcing culture—and good sales managers are discovering that the best way to leverage their efforts is to manage the culture.

MANAGING THE CULTURE: THE FIVE FACTORS OF HIGH PERFORMANCE

After more than ten years of research we've come up with five factors that are critical to creating and maintaining a high-performance work culture.

Listed in order of importance, they are:

1. A Shared Sense of Mission or Purpose. This is the critical factor and the factor that is so much a part of this book. It's the culture equivalent to purpose. It answers the questions "What's expected around here, what do we do and *why* do we do it?" If the only answer that you have is "Making money," be prepared for your people to ask for as much as they can get for doing as little as they can. On the other hand, if you've taken the time to establish a mission—and especially if you've taken the time to involve your people in the process—that larger sense of mission will help people focus on achieving their part of the mission.

Be prepared to sell and promote that mission as often as possible. This means that at your formal and informal sales meetings you don't talk just about sales made and dollars brought in. Get your people talking about problems that were solved and clients who benefited. Those are the good-news war stories that stir souls. Remember, people want to do significant things. Typically what they are looking for is *permission* from their manager and their culture to make significance a part of their job and their life.

2. Have Clear and Attainable Goals. People perform best when they have specific goals. Goals that are reachable yet that stretch them. This is not telling people what to do, or how to do it, but it's giving them the map, the destination and sometimes the general direction in which to start.

3. Frequent Objective Feedback. No one works well in a vacuum, or in highly ambiguous situations where they don't know how they're doing. People learn quickly and work well when they are told how they're doing. Debrief and summarize every joint call you make. Don't assume that people know how they're doing or know what you think. Lead with positive information first, but always be honest, objective and specific. Help your people learn from every selling experience.

4. Positive Rewards for Appropriate or Approximate Performance. Selling is like playing tennis: very few people get it right the first time. If you waited for a brand-new player to win a match before you rewarded him, you'd end with a frustrated, unmotivated and discouraged player—if he didn't quit or "fail" first. Instead, every time he does something right—the first volley, the first backhand that looks approximately right—that's the time to reward. Sincere, positive reinforcement—"You did that really well," "You really understand this," "You're doing a great job"—is a most important factor in helping people learn. It's catching people doing something right and telling them about it.

5. Timely Support and Help When Requested or Needed. This is an issue of priorities for most sales managers. It's deciding what your job is. Are you there to track numbers and quotas, or are you there to support your people? Clearly, both jobs have to be done, but the job of coach is the critical job in creating a high-performance team. That means, within realistic boundaries, being there when needed, playing the supporting role. Sometimes it means being more concerned with what a salesperson is learning than with whether a sale is being made. For example, many a sales manager has sat in on a joint call with a new salesperson and fidgeted internally as the salesperson struggled with a presentation or with objections. The natural instinct is to jump in and take over. The problem is that when you do that, learning stops. Nothing teaches selling better than real-world mistakes, setbacks, screw-ups and glitches. But, as sales managers, when we have our coaching hats on we have to allow those mistakes and setbacks to happen. Then we have to make sure our people learn from the experiences.

THE FIVE FACTORS OF HIGH PERFORMANCE

1. A shared sense of mission or purpose.
2. Having clear and attainable goals.
3. Receiving frequent, objective feedback.
4. Receiving positive rewards for appropriate or approximate performance.
5. Receiving timely support and help when requested or needed.

The Five Factors and Performance

Wayne Townsend, the manager of sales education and training for GM of Canada, has worked extensively with us on using the five factors to help make positive changes in the cultures of GM dealerships. Wayne sees the results in two ways. The first is subjective. As Wayne puts it, you can visit two dealerships that are across the street from each other. In the first dealership, with a healthy reinforcing culture, you can feel the energy, the synergy of what's going on. You can see it in the customers and in the sales and service people. Then you walk across the street—where the culture is not working for the dealership or the manager—and you see the exact opposite story.

But there is more going on than just subjective indicators. In a study that GM and Wilson Learning did of dealerships in Halifax, we found a very high correlation between the five factors—a positive healthy culture—and productivity and performance.

Wayne will tell you that culture, productivity and performance are inseparable, and that's why more and more managers are becoming managers of their culture.

ATTENTION, PATIENCE AND TOUGH DECISIONS

It takes time, effort, truth and balance to come up with a high-performing sales team. It takes paying attention to it, being patient during its development. Pay attention to it *especially* when times are tough, when your team is behind quota; that's when it really counts. You have to have the courage to stick to your selling purpose. Keep saying, "Help our clients solve their problems" when your gut is telling you that you absolutely need to make some sales.

There will be some people who will not get it, who will not understand or accept the purpose of the work unit. One or two people who do not have a sense of integrity or who are caught in the old adversarial mindset can do a lot of damage to your group's long-term reputation and its effectiveness. What to do about those people will be a hard decision for you. But you will have only one choice. To paraphrase John Allison of Branch Banking and Trust of North Carolina, that choice will be to terminate them with great mercy—*even if in the short term they are high performers.* Tough, but necessary.

DOUBLE BIND

An important word of caution. People always understand what they get paid to do, and then they usually go out and do it. By that I mean that no matter what the "lip service" mission of the organization is, no matter what is stamped on the bottom of every memo, we are all adept at picking up "the truth" no matter what is being said. In psychology this can lead to what is called the double bind—double messages. For example, many companies and many sales managers give lip service to a "customer-first" orientation, then those same managers spend most of their time and attention on the numbers, on quota, and on margins. The message to the sales force, to every one who works for the company, is clear: It's the numbers, the quotas and the margins that are important, not the clients; clients are simply a means to right numbers, quotas and margins.

Here's a suggestion. Write this out and display it where you can see it every day:

"YOUR RESULTS ARE BASED ON WHAT YOU PAY ATTENTION TO."

It's an old saw, but if you want a sales force that values customer focus, that believes they get paid for serving clients, you, your boss and the organization have to act that way. You *have to pay attention* to those things. The culture has to be consistent, otherwise people get double messages and they always act on what the truth is, on what they get reinforced for. You always get what you reinforce. The problem is that sometimes we're not sure what the culture is reinforcing.

I remember attending a meeting in which a manager was talking about innovation. He was attempting to "sell" his work unit on a belief that their mission was to take the time and the energy to develop the leading-edge products in their particular field. But every five minutes or so someone from the group would ask about margins, or about timelines, or ask the increasingly perplexed manager if he really meant what he was saying. It was obvious to me that the manager sincerely meant what he was talking about. But when you dug into the culture a little bit, you discovered that for the previous two years the stated and unstated mission of this particular work group had been to crank out product on cost and on time, to replicate, not innovate. It was when the profit margins were on target that celebrations occurred or bonuses came about. Creativity, because it interfered with timelines and with margin, was, in reality, discouraged. So even though the manager was sincere about innovation, it was obvious why his people didn't believe him and, to his frustration, why they adopted a wait-and-see attitude. He was saying one thing, but the culture of the organization had traditionally given a totally different message. Double bind.

Balance

The solution is not to give up paying attention to profits. You're probably relieved to hear that. The solution is balance. To quote John Allison again, "Our mission is to serve our clients and survive and grow economically. We tell our clients that. You have to have the economic mission and the purpose mission in balance." Get out of kilter either way and your employees pick it up and act accordingly.

It is probably fair to say that most sales managers are out of balance toward the economic mission. The challenge is to begin to pay more attention to the purpose mission, to bring it back into balance.

THE IMPORTANCE OF BEING A SALES MANAGER

Even as you look at all the changes going on in sales management, there is clearly one thing that hasn't changed: the importance of the sales manager's role. No one else plays a more critical role in the development of salespersons, in their performance level and in the longevity of each salesperson.

At the Pecos River Learning Center, we've learned this lesson a number of times. After some heroic attempts, we've learned that you cannot even train salespeople unless you train and involve the sales managers. It *always* goes hand in hand. You can have the best sales training money can buy, the most empowered new salesperson possible, but the moment he or she steps back into the office, if that manager doesn't support it or doesn't understand it, it's only a matter of time before the training is lost. Managers, whether they do it consciously or not, *are* the support system. They are the most important persons on the support team.

So, finally, I want to acknowledge the importance of sales managers. If I wanted to do a quick check on the health and future of a company, sales managers are the barometer that I'd use. If they were discouraged, cynical and defeated, no matter what the executives in the home office said, or what the financial people said, I'd be very pessimistic. But show me a group of sales managers who are excited, turned on and in charge—that's the kind of company that gets my attention.

Sales managers are the link between corporate mission and implementation of that mission with clients. They, more than any other group of professionals in the organization, are responsible not only for high performance but also for issues with long-term strategic impact, like corporate integrity and client focus. An organization cannot go wrong spending money empowering, training and celebrating sales managers, especially organizations going through phase change or coming to grips with new market conditions.

Because nothing changes in selling unless sales management changes.

Managing the Phase III Sales Team Summary

Managing with the gun is the old game. Managing with the kind word—influence and personal power instead of position power—is the new game of sales management.

Thinking Shift: Imagine that you have two groups of clients. One is comprised of the people who buy your products and services. The other group of clients is the salespeople who work for you. As managers, we need to learn how to sell "work."

Have a work culture meeting. Get your people sharing their feelings and thoughts about the culture, about work—talking about why they work, what they're looking for, what their frustrations are and what you can do to help. As a manager, just listen. Help your people develop, stick to and reinforce a balanced economic and purpose mission statement.

Use the Five Factors of High Performance to keep your team on track:

1. A shared sense of mission or purpose.
2. Having clear and attainable goals.
3. Receiving frequent, objective feedback.
4. Receiving positive rewards for appropriate or approximate performance.
5. Receiving timely support and help when requested or needed.

Beware of the double bind. Do some soul searching. What is the real message you're trying to get across? Work on constancy and consistency and balance.

AFTERWORD

JOURNEY'S END

A final principle and a story to wrap this up. The principle is about how to begin effectively using the Strategic Thought Process in your work. Call it the "No Magic Pill" Principle—there are not shortcuts to learning new ways of thinking. There are no magic pills. How we learn is simple to understand, but it takes conscious effort and attention from the learner.

Here is a simple learning model. It's something we all know, have all experienced—it belongs in the realm of common sense: *What you learn, practice. What you practice becomes habit. What becomes habit becomes your results.*

For example, practice every day, every sales call, telling yourself that your purpose is to help your clients get what they want. Practice it until it becomes habit, until it's automatic. Once it's automatic, it's part of you—it's effortless, like tying your shoes. And of course the trade-off is that this kind of outward focus can dramatically and positively affect your success and fulfillment in selling. Not a bad deal for a little effort up front.

But it takes that effort up front.

Next, Ann Spinazzola of NorthWestern Mutual has a saying: "A closed mind is an expensive thing." A closed mind says, "This will never work," or "I tried it once and nothing happened, so forget it," or "I'm not going to try that and risk making a mistake in front of a client." All of those postures eliminate the possibility to really learn. Learning new ways of thinking takes patience, an open and exploring mind—the posture of the learner instead of the learned. So give yourself permission to learn, to try things out, to make mistakes, to have setbacks. That's the natural process; sometimes we just have to get ourselves—our egos—out of the way.

Now the story. Ronn Lehmann, writer and consultant to the Pecos River Learning Center, has spent much of his time in the last ten years out on the road interviewing and riding with salespeople and sales managers. The incidents that follow took place at an automobile dealership in Southern California where he spent two weeks learning about the operation and the salespeople:

A salesperson whom Ronn was observing one day was obviously having trouble closing a sale with an elderly couple. The couple were angry—so much so that they finally got up from the table and walked out the door. The salesperson, also upset, walked over to where Ronn was sitting, sighed deeply and confided, in all seriousness and as if bestowing a great truth, that the reason he hadn't made the sale was that the couple were Armenian —he could sell to anybody else, he said, but had never had any luck with Armenians.

That tells you a little bit about "culture." But fortunately for Ronn's sanity one of the other salespeople Ronn interviewed was a young woman, intelligent, good people skills, a go getter and brand-new to the dealership. She had gone through her one-week orientation, she had been on the floor for another week and had just made her first sale. She was enthusiastic and she loved what she was doing. She talked about really getting to know her customers, about making sure they got exactly what they wanted, about not pressuring them and about establishing friendships. She was bubbling over, talking about much of the Phase III stuff that we've looked at in this book.

About half way through the interview, an older, more "experienced" salesperson stopped to listen. He let her go on for a while longer. Then he cut her short. He told her that she didn't understand the business, that the only way to succeed in this business was to get customers to the closing table and grind them. That was how you made sales, he said—they were the enemy and this was war, and never forget it. Then he walked away.

The reaction was almost as if someone had turned a light switch off. She closed up, you could see that she began automatically to question her early beliefs. That's how fast it can happen.

What's the point? The first point is that, just like the saleswoman, we all know most of what's been covered in this journey. Some of the material is sophisticated— partnering, leadership and leveraging, for example. But the other important ideas, like helping others get what they want, getting your ego out of the way, and value added—wanting to exceed your customer's expectations —are anything but new and sophisticated. Everybody in selling, especially new people, wants to work that way. The new woman in the dealership was an example of that. Sometimes all we need is a little support to begin with.

The second point is that many of us have obstacles— dragons—to overcome in order to work the way we want to work. For the woman in the dealership the obstacle was the culture in the dealership. For the rest of us, it might be a similar problem or it might be our own egos and their fear of change. Either way, it might take a little courage, some healthy self-talk and that first small step in order to get on the road that leads to those feelings of fulfillment and the success that is shared by the game changers.

But the good news is that all of us as salespeople—like the woman in the dealership—are naturally game changers. All it takes, sometimes, is permission from ourselves, support from ourselves, and sometimes a small leap to catch the next trapeze.

If you wish further information about *Changing the Game* courses or about Larry Wilson and the Pecos River Learning Center, you may contact:

The Pecos River Learning Center
1660 Old Pecos Trail, Suite H
Santa Fe, NM 87501
(505) 989-9101

accountability, 174, 209, 210, 237
Addressograph-Multigraph, 38–40
adequate solution, 70–72
Aha! (Gardner), 152
Ainsworth-Land, George, 30–51
Air Midwest, 34–35
alignment, 191–92
Allison, John, 129, 137, 202–3, 272, 274
American Can, 25
American Physicians Service Company, 241
AM International, 39
anticipation, 24–26
tool for, *see* Growth Model
Apple Computer, 23, 46–47
Archimedes, 226
arrogance, 41–42
assistants, 229–30
AT&T, 261
Austin, Nancy, 43, 251

Banta, Merle, 39
"Be Back," 57–58, 184

beliefs:
power of, 109–10
strategy for changing, 110–115
Bennis, Warren, 166
"Big Q" quality, 48
Bradbury, Ray, 156
Braslow, Alan, 19, 100, 123, 142, 163, 207, 215
Breckenridge, Charles, 99, 143, 235
burn-the-boat strategy, 156
Business and Commercial Aviation, 147*n*
Business Week, 64
buying power, of women, 252–253

Cadette, Walter, 265
Carlson, Eric, 92, 100, 161
Challenge Cup, 154–55
Challenger, 42
Change (Watzlawick, Weakland & Fisch), 27*n*
commitment, 267
of purpose, 129–34

commitment (*cont.*)
  to service, 130
  to vision, 155–57
communication, in leadership,
    169–73, 176
Coolidge, Calvin, 130
Coronado, 156
courage, 102, 120–22, 174
Cray, Seymour, 150–51, 156
Cray Research, 45–46, 150–51
creativity, 91, 141–59
  blocks to, 147–48
  offline thinking and, 150–53
  sparking of, 148–50
  steps of, 147–58
  trust in, 152–53
  of value-added service, 203–
    204, 205
  visualization and, 144–47, 153–
    155
Crystal, John, 132–33

Death of a Salesman (Miller),
    13
debugging principle, 157
decision-makers, multiple, 53–
    55
deep breathing, 112
demassification, 61–62
Democracy in America
    (Tocqueville), 249
Depression, Great, 138–39
Donoghue, Bob, 212
double bind, 272–73
Drucker, Peter, 24–25, 72, 143,
    266
Du Pont, 61

ego, 107–8
  letting go of, 116–20
80/20 rule, 227
Einstein, Albert, 149
Electronic Data Systems, 47
EMBER (establishing mutually
    beneficial, empathic
    relationships), 184–89

empowerment, 173–74, 176
entrepreneurs, 33–35, 239–41
evolution, change through, 23–
    24

failure, 38–40, 81, 90–91
  disbelief in, 102–23
  fear of, 102, 104–9
failure-success line, 85–87
Federal Express Corporation,
    48, 120–21
feedback, 269–70
Fisch, Richard, 27*n*
Flis, Diane, 19, 99, 126, 134,
    154, 187–88, 206, 216, 218,
    238, 253
Frankl, Victor, 84–87,114
Fraternal Life Insurance
    Company, 224
Freiden Calculators, 38–40
fulfillment, 86–87, 104–5
fulfillment-depression line, 84–
    87
funnel, inverted, 230–34
future shock, 29

game change, 24–28
  letting go in, 26–27
  personal, 26
Game Change Principle, 27
Gardner, Martin, 152
General Motors, 25, 47
geometric thinking, 225–26
GLO (generalized leverageable
    opportunity), 239–40
goals, 269
Gove, Bill, 144–45
Grayson, Art, 173–74, 175–77,
    210
Grow or Die (Ainsworth-Land),
    30
Growth Model, 30–51
  "phase blindness" and, 32
  Phase I, 33–35
  Phase II, 35–44
  Phase III, 44–50

Gulfstream Corporation, 64–67
Gumucio, Marcelo, 45–46, 204–205, 207, 266

Hailey, Walter, 239–40
Haldane, J. B. S., 37–38
Hamilton, Alexander, 39
Harman, Willis, 146
Hewlett-Packard, 39–40
Higher Creativity (Harman), 146
Hoffer, Eric, 158
Hope, Bob, 153
Hughes Aircraft, 47
Hultgren, Gary, 73–74

IBM, 64–65, 71–72
Ickx, Jackie, 168–69
immune system, of organizations, 42–44
innovation, 24–26, 32, 46–47, 273–74
integration, 47–48
International Young Presidents Organization, 84
interpersonal value added, 209–212

Jobs, Steven, 46–47
Johns, David, 48
Judson, H. F., 37

Kennedy, Edward M., 172
Kimery, Ray, 194–96
Kline, Morris, 152n
know-how, learn-how vs., 158
Kraft, Inc., 193–96

Labor Statistics, Bureau of, 264
Larsen, Earnie, 121–22
Leaders (Bennis), 166
leadership, 160–79, 188–89
    characteristics of, 166–77

communication in, 169–73, 176
empowerment in, 173–74, 176
motives for, 164–65
myth of, 164–65
positive intent of, 165–66
vision in, 166–73, 175–76
"walking the talk" in, 174, 176–77
Lear, Bill, 146–47
learn-how, know-how vs., 158
Lehmann, Ronn, 278–79
Leider, Dick, 127–28, 227
leveraging, 57–58, 223–43
    assistants and, 229–30
    audit for, 227–28
    geometric thinking in, 225–226
    GLO in, 239–40
    high-level, 239–40
    ideas for, 226–38
    NEER in, 241
    networks for, 234–36
    principle of, 226
    prospecting and, 230–34
    referrals and repeats from, 237–38
    strategic plan for, 226–30
lip service, 272–73
Lone Star Life, 239
Long, Newton, 70
long-term thinking, 184–88

MacArthur, Douglas, 198–99
McGeary, Marion, 253
McMahon, David, 241
Mann, Larry, 18, 92, 99, 103, 125, 200
Man's Search for Meaning (Frankl), 84, 114
Mazda, 213–14
Messinger, Jay, 132, 153
Milliken and Company, 218–21
Million Dollar Round Table, 144
Minnesota Twins, 121–22
Montague, Ashley, 247, 256

Montgomery and Andrews, 170–172
Monthei, Kathy, 19, 100, 116, 131, 154, 230, 257, 258
Moore Business Forms and Systems Division, 73–74
Morton-Thiokol, 42
Motorola, 25
Murphy, Jack, 241
Music Man, The (Willson), 13
myth, leadership, 164–65

NASA, 42
National Association of Life Underwriters, 145–46
Natural Superiority of Women, The (Montague), 247, 256
Nautilus, 174
NEC (Nihon Electric Company), 235–36
NEER (naturally existing economic relationship), 241
networking, 234–36
"never enough" game, 83–84, 88
New England Life, 47
Nietzsche, Friedrich, 105
Nightengale, Earl, 211
"No Magic Pill" Principle, 277
North Carolina Branch Banking and Trust Company, 136–38
Nygaard, Mary, 261–63

offline thinking, 150–53
Oklahoma, University of, 240
organizational drift, 40–41
Organizational Drift, 40
organizations:
Phase I, 33–35
Phase II, 35–44
Phase III, 44–49, 52–76

partnering, 62–65, 180–97
alignment in, 191–92

EMBER in, 184–89
keys to, 189–96
long-term thinking in, 184–88
shared values in, 189–91
strategic advantage of, 182–84
support in, 191, 192–93
TASTE in, 190–91

Passion for Excellence (Peters & Austin), 43, 251
Pecos River Learning Center, 25–26, 117–20, 190–91, 275
Peters, Tom, 43, 251
phase blind, 32
Phase I organizations, 33–35
Phase I salespeople, 78–82, 180
Phase II organizations, 35–44
arrogance of, 41–42
immune system of, 42–44
organizational drift in, 40–41
transition to, 36–37
Phase II salespeople, 82–87, 181
"never enough" game of, 83–84, 88
Phase III organizations, 44–50, 52–76
buyer-seller relationship in, 62–65, 68, 92; *see also* partnering
demassification in, 61–62
different languages in, 54–55
innovation in, 46–47
integration in, 47–48
multiple decision-makers in, 53–55
product solution in, 65–69
quality in, 48
random events in, 58–61
as running awake, 44–46
Phase III salespeople, 87–93
characteristics of, 89–93
client relationships of, 92; *see also* partnering
creativity of, 91; *see also* creativity

fulfillment of, 87
motivation of, 89–90
outward focus of, 91, 131–32
purposefulness of, 125–26
strategic thinking of, 91
as team players, 92
Pillsbury, 193–96
Porsche, 142–43, 149–50, 167–169
Pound, John, 170–72
Power of Purpose, The (Lieder), 128
Procter and Gamble, 80
productivity, 257–58
product solution, 53, 65–69
prospecting, 80, 230–34
purpose, partnership, 191
purpose, selling, 124–40, 165, 268–69
    commitments of, 129–34
    outward focus in, 131–32
    power of, 127–28

quality, 48, 89

Rampey, John, 219
random events, 58–61
referrals, 182–84, 213; *see also* leveraging
Rickover, Hyman, 174
Rogers, Will, 24
running awake, 44–45, 52

sales cycle, 55–58
sales managers, 79, 261–78
    double messages from, 272–73
    establishment of mission by, 268–69
    feedback from, 269–70
    goal-setting by, 269
    importance of, 274–75
    interpersonal skills of, 263–66
    rewards from, 270
    role of, 261–63
    salespeople and, 266–67
    support from, 270–71
    work culture and, 268–71
salespeople, 77–102
    as partners, 62–65; *see also* partnering
    Phase I, 78–82, 180
    Phase II, 82–88, 181
    Phase III, *see* Phase III salespeople
    women as, 249–60
Schmitt, Stan, 61, 181–82
Schoenthaler, Brian, 34–35
Schutz, Peter, 142–43, 149–50, 167–69
Scientific American, 156n
Search For Solutions, The (Judson), 37
Sears, 62
self-talk, 110–13
    challenging, 112–13
    listening to, 110–11
selling:
    changes in, 21–22
    creativity of, 91, 141–59
    "feminine" abilities in, 255–57
    freedom of, 258–59
    leadership in, 160–79, 188–89
    through leveraging, 223–43
    new rules in, 21–22, 52–76
    "outside the nine dots," 87–89
    partnering in, 180–97
    productivity of, 257–58
    purpose of, 124–40, 165
    three Cs of, 22
    value added service in, 71, 198–222
    women in, 249–60
service, commitment to, 130–32
Sherber, Tony, 194–96
shock, change through, 22–23
Smith, Fred, 120–21, 144
SouthWest Airlines, 35
Spinazzola, Ann, 19, 89, 100–101, 127, 133, 153, 166, 184,

Spinazzola, Ann (*cont.*)
208, 230, 234, 250, 254, 258, 278
Steele, Peggy, 256
Stevens, David, 121–22
"Strangest Secret, The," 211
Strommen, Clair, 224
Studebaker, Paul, 212
support, 191, 192–93, 270–71
Sutton, Willy, 264
Suzuki, Yoshitaka, 235–36

talent, individual, 132–34
TASTE (trust, accountability, support, truth, effort), 190–191
teamwork, 74, 92, 162–63, 165–166, 217–18, 267–68
"Ten Like Me" (film), 83
Tertocha, Eileen, 20, 101, 126, 132, 135, 202, 233, 258
Time, 265
time management, 74
Tocqueville, Alexis de, 249
Toffler, Alvin, 29, 61
Townsend, Wayne, 68, 271
Toyota, 47
True, Herb, 145
trust, 152–53, 183–84, 191, 192–193

US West, 261–63

value added, 71, 198–222
in automobile sales, 205–6, 210
big picture in, 205–6
competitive edge of, 200–201
creativity of, 203–4, 205
defining, 201–3
evaluation of, 206–7
in financial services, 212
in human-resource services, 206–7
interpersonal, 209–12
in life insurance, 208
problems and, 212–17
in real estate, 201–2
steps of, 203–8
in supercomputers, 207–8
teamwork in, 217–18
understanding your business and, 204–5
values, shared, 189–91
vision, 141–59
alignment on, 191–92
commitment to, 155–57
debugging principle and, 157
in leadership, 166–73, 175–76
sparking of, 148–50
trust in, 152–53
visualization, 144–47, 153–55

Walker, Don, 80, 101, 161, 170, 193, 204, 235
walking the talk, 174, 176–77
Wanamaker, John, 226–27
Watzlawick, Paul, 27*n*
Weakland, John, 27*n*
Weisz, Bill, 45
Wilhelm, Mike, 90, 186
Wilkinson, Bud, 240
Wilson Learning Corporation, 40, 56, 59–60, 71, 83, 86–87, 189–90, 226
women, 249–60
as customers, 252–54
selling talents of, 255–57
work culture, 268–71

Yamamoto, Shinichi, 213–14